Miracle Herbal Cures

Dr. Michael L. McCann D.Ed., N.D.

Miracle Herbal Cures
by Dr. Michael L. McCann, D.Ed., N.D.
Pneuma Life Publishing
4423 Forbes Blvd
Lanham, MD 20706
www.pneumalife.com

This book or parts thereof may not be reproduced in any form, stored in a retrieval system or transmitted in any form by any means—electronic, mechanical, photocopy, recording or otherwise—without prior written permission of the publisher, except as provided by United States of America copyright law.

Unless otherwise noted, Scripture quotations are from the King James Version of the Bible.

All Scripture quotations marked NIV are from the Holy Bible New International Version. Copyright © 1973, 1978, 1984, International Bible Society. Used by permission.

Copyright © 2001 by Dr. Michael L. McCann
All rights reserved
ISBN: 1-56229-166-1
Printed in the United States of America

DISCLAIMER

Much of the advice in this book is based upon the research, professional and personal experiences of the author. If the reader has any questions concerning any material or procedure mentioned, the author strongly suggests seeking the advice of a physician or professional health care practitioner. The advice of a health care practitioner as well as proper medical screening should precede the start of any new diet, supplement or treatment program. Some of the treatments and suggestions mentioned in this book may have different effects on different people. The author is not liable for any advice, effects or consequences resulting from the use or misuse of any procedures, materials or preparations suggested in this book. The author believes that this information can be helpful to the general public.

Contents

Introduction 7

Chapter One
God's Way of Healthy Living 13

Chapter Two
Using Herbs Wisely 29

Chapter Three
Strengthening the Heart 41

Chapter Four
*High Blood Pressure
and Blood Cleansing* 49

Chapter Five
God's Little Liver Pills 57

Chapter Six
*Osteoporosis:
The Case of the Shrinking Human* 65

Chapter Seven
New Hope for the Diabetic 73

Chapter Eight
God's Natural Prozac 81

Miraculous Herbal Cures

Chapter Nine
God's Miracle Cure for the Prostate 89

Chapter Ten
God's Natural Aspirin 95

Chapter Eleven
God's Best Herbs for Anxiety 103

Chapter Twelve
Helpful Herbs for Allergies 111

Chapter Thirteen
The Miracle of Licorice 117

Chapter Fourteen
God's Natural Healing for Asthma 125

Chapter Fifteen
God's Cure for the Common Cold 133

Chapter Sixteen
God's Natural Relief From Stress 141

Chapter Seventeen
Natural Help for Arthritis 147

Chapter Eighteen
Putting It All Together 155

Notes 162

Introduction

In the past twenty-five years, there has been a growing interest in the use of herbs as natural medicine. Most of the twentieth century did not give us a great variety of medications for the healing of countless diseases. Many times over-the-counter and doctor-prescribed medications produced severe reactions, and in many cases, the cure has been worse than the disease. Many of us were not aware of other options, but thank God that this is changing.

At last in the United States herbal products, homeopathic remedies and other alternative medicines are becoming more available at a reasonable price. We are now able to find natural products just about everywhere.

Miracle Herbal Cures

Flus, pneumonia, tuberculosis, typhoid and other serious infections were the leading cause of death seventy years ago, but today these are very rare due to the use of advanced antibiotics. Many still turn to pills for a quick treatment at the onset of an illness. Americans in particular have put much faith in pills. When you take into consideration the results of antibiotics in the treatment of infections, the natural inclination is to take pills. The only problem facing us today is that antibiotics are becoming less effective because bacteria are becoming more resistant to them.

According to the Public Health Service, the United States is facing a major health care crisis due to our continued reliance on man-made drugs, radiation and surgery. There are bacteria that have become so strong that even antibiotics can't touch them. Another crisis we are about to face is the debilitating chronic degenerative diseases such as: arthritis, chronic pain, allergies, diabetes, viral infections, depression, mental illness, colitis, multiple sclerosis, cancer and cardiovascular disease. Man-made medications are not the most effective for the treatment of these diseases.

It is time we start preventing illness instead of trying to cure an illness. In the 1994 report "Alternative Medicine: Expanding Medical Horizons," the Public Health Service states "many health problems today require multimodal treatment and prevention approaches." To put it bluntly, there aren't enough pills to cure what truly ails us. We must understand that we have to go beyond pills, radiation and surgery. This means that we must come back to God's way of healing.

Introduction

Our heavenly Father has provided us with thousands of herbs that can be very effective in the prevention and treatment of disease.

Natural healing is becoming very popular in the United States. At the same time natural and herbal healing has been used in Europe and the rest of the world for centuries. At last Americans are realizing that the spirit, soul and body must come into focus if true and lasting health is achieved. God has always taken into consideration the whole man when He heals. Spiritual factors, mental factors and physical factors are all pertinent to the holistic healer.

Just a few years ago acupuncture, massage, guided imagery, homeopathy and even chiropractic were considered on the "lunatic fringe." Today we now know these modalities do have a very important place in healing.

Just as it was practiced in the Bible, natural healing is greatly involved in the prevention of disease. Natural healing stresses prenatal care, regular checkups, blood pressure screening, cholesterol testing and following a regime of proper diet and exercise. Conventional medicine offers very few means of prevention.

The National Institute of Health established the Office of Alternative Medicine in the 1990s. Today even the American Cancer Society recognizes alternative therapies as being legitimate.

Let us not forget that the United States turned its back on natural remedies and herbs even though the rest of the world did not. Foreign medical journals are reporting new remedies found in plants and herbs. The British and Germans are leading

Miracle Herbal Cures

the pack for the use of alternative medicine. In China, alternative medicine is used extensively. The Chinese have over 5,800 plants from which they make their medicines. It is interesting to note that in Germany herbal remedies are sold over-the-counter with other drugs side by side. The medical profession in Germany recognizes no less than 300 herbs with more being added.

Herbs, at one particular time, were the stuff of folk medicine and old wives' tales. Not so today as research has shown that herbs *do* have tremendous healing propensities. Scientists are looking for new cures for cancer and heart disease from the properties found in numerous herbs.

Heart disease, cancer, respiratory disease, liver disease and diabetes are still the leading cause of death in Western society. Modern medicine does very little to prevent these particular diseases. On the other hand, herbs can help prevent all of the above.

There is a most outstanding list of herbs that can heal and prevent numerous diseases. Many of them are found in Scripture.

We know that garlic can prevent heart disease since it lowers overall total cholesterol and triglycerides. It also boosts the good cholesterol, HDL, while lowering the bad cholesterol, LDL. Garlic acts as an antibiotic killing both bacteria, certain viruses and fungi.

It is now known that ginger root dissolves the type of blood clots responsible for heart attacks and strokes just as well as aspirin. The Food and Drug Administration (FDA) approved aspirin in the prevention and treatment of coronaries. The only

Introduction

problem with this is that aspirin kills off the flora and fauna that help make vitamin K, which is produced in the colon. There are several herbs that function as immune enhancers such as echinacea, astragalus and ginseng. Milk Thistle is known to protect and heal the liver from damage due to alcohol and a wide variety of drugs. Saw palmetto is known to prevent and stop prostate disease. There are literally countless herbs that function almost miraculously in the human body.

There are very few side effects from taking herbs, if any. At the same time there are some herbs that are "deadly" and should not be taken at all. The herbs that will be examined in this book may be purchased at health food stores, K-Mart, Target, Walgreens and Wal-Mart. These all come with very easy instructions on how to take them.

Herbs are very powerful medicines and must be taken with great care. It is best to take them only when you are ill or for the purpose of prevention. With my patients I recommend they look for all natural products that are synergistic. Synergistic herbs and vitamins all work together without causing side effects. These will provide you with wonderful benefits at the least numbers of tablets or capsules to take. At the same time these will be the best at the least cost to you. Try to discover the side effects of the herbs before casually taking them. If you arm yourself with this information first, you will be greatly blessed.

So many people complain of being tired, but the use of the proper herbs will revitalize their energy. Once this happens you don't ever have to be tired again.

Miracle Herbal Cures

The purpose of this book is to help you regain your health and maintain good health. We will discuss various diseases and the herbs that aid in a cure, but do not try to diagnose yourself. Truly the use of herbs can be totally miraculous as we see their outstanding results. It is my personal belief that the body will heal itself if it is given the proper nutrients and herbs. With this belief in mind, I have set out to provide you with the vital information to bring about positive results in your health.

Chapter One

God's Way of Healthy Living

As we follow God's Word we live healthy and fulfilling lives. One of the ways we can do this is to know how to keep our bodies healthy. The Bible has a great deal to tell us about eating and living healthy lives.

When people choose to live disorderly lives and unhealthy eating habits, their lives can only lead to unhappiness for themselves and those around them.

The Bible is our guidebook for living healthy and orderly lives. The Bible tells us of certain herbs and their benefits. It also speaks of the healthiest food we can eat. When we follow the simplest method of eating, as found in the Bible, we will live healthier and more peaceful lives.

LISTEN TO YOUR FATHER

In the Old Testament, God appeared as a disciplinarian Father who laid down the rules and severely punished those who disobeyed them.

In the New Testament, Jesus Christ gives us the reasons for the rules and regulations. Here God is seen as a loving and merciful Father who wants to enter into fellowship with us so that we won't punish or destroy ourselves.

Jesus showed us a better way to live. He summed up the Ten Commandments by giving us the greatest of all commandments: "Thou shalt love the Lord thy God with all thy heart, and with all thy soul, and with all thy mind. This is the first and great commandment. And the second is like unto it, Thou shalt love thy neighbour as thyself. On these two commandments hang all the law and the prophets" (Matt. 22:37-40). These two commandments require us to love our God and our neighbor as ourselves. We are to accept the will of God and His way of life even as a child. All of God's commandments found in Scripture aim at helping us live healthy and happy lives in the here and now. In so doing, we will gain heaven.

THE BIBLE AND FOOD FACTS

The Bible is not a diet-and-nutrition book. It isn't a health and fitness "how-to" book. It isn't filled with recipes or menus to assist in preparing the right kind of foods.

There are no exercise programs found within the Scriptures. There are no set rules about shaping your muscles and body parts. But it is a book about people living healthy and happy lives. As we note the types of herbs and foods that they ate, we can learn how to better take care of our bodies so that they will be in excellent shape. Our minds will become sharper and more active.

From Genesis to Revelation, just about every book of the Bible contains references to foods of the day and herbs that were used abundantly. It also speaks of rules governing their cultivation, preparation and consumption. In Genesis, God said:

> "Let the earth bring forth grass, the herb yielding seed, and the fruit tree yielding fruit after his kind whose seed is in itself, upon the earth; and it was so....I have given you every herb bearing seed, which is upon the face of all the earth, and every tree, in the which is the fruit of a tree yielding seed, to you it shall be for meat."
>
> —Genesis 1:11, 29

Even the final book of the Bible—Revelation—speaks of flowing fruit trees. "In the midst of the street of it, and on either side of the river, was there the tree of life, which bare twelve manner of fruits, and yielded her fruit every month: and the leaves of the tree were for the healing of the nations" (Rev. 22:2).

Although scholars have been studying the foods of the Bible for centuries, it is only recently that modern-day nutritionists have discovered biblical

Miracle Herbal Cures

foods and herbs are very good for people today. In my opinion, we could greatly benefit from eating some of these foods.

The cuisine that is found in the Bible is incredibly healthy. No modern-day nutritionist would question the validity of eating such a diet. Their diet encouraged good health and many of the foods contained herbs that actually combated disease. Modern scientists have discovered numerous foods that do help prevent cancer, heart disease and other serious illnesses.

These people of the Bible followed the dietary laws of the Talmud, which told how to prepare certain foods and what foods to avoid. The Jews used plants for medicinal purposes, which was an accepted custom. The Book of Proverbs tells about the lifestyle of God's people when "the herbs of the mountains are gathered in" (Prov. 27:25). Biblical people did not know of diabetes since they never used white sugar. They would use honey as a sweetener or the pulps of fresh fruits.

These folks ate grapes, figs, pomegranates, dates, cucumbers, small carrots, beans, lentils and numerous herbs such as dill, cumin, coriander, mint, turmeric, cinnamon, bark, saffron, mustard, rue and a bitter herb that might have been a type of wild endive.

Because there are literally hundreds of references to plants in the Scriptures, it is impossible to cover them all in this writing. But in the following pages we will speak of herbs that were found in the Bible and used during Biblical times. These were used to fight diseases and maintain good health as well as for daily sustenance. Many of these can be found at your local supermarket or health food store.

> "And by the river upon the bank thereof, on this side and on that side, shall grow all trees for meat, whose leaf shall not fade, neither shall the fruit thereof be consumed: it shall bring forth new fruit according to his months, because their waters they issued out of the sanctuary: and the fruit thereof shall be for meat, and the leaf thereof for medicine."
>
> —Ezekiel 47:12

The Israelites ate very simple foods prepared with herbs that kept them healthy. Their diet consisted mainly of bread, fruits and vegetables. These foods contained the needed fiber now recognized by our medical profession to fend off both the ravages of aging and a host of degenerative diseases.

In addition to a healthy diet, people during Bible times walked everywhere, unlike the modern modes of transportation that we use today.

WHEN IN ROME, DON'T DO AS THE ROMANS

Biblical living was very simple living and totally natural. It was life as God intended it to be. At the same time other cultures did not live by the same guidelines as the Israelites. For instance, the Romans were not a picture of sparkling good health.

Upper-class Romans lived quite differently than Israelites. It is interesting to note that we suffer

Miracle Herbal Cures

from many of the same degenerative diseases that the Romans suffered.

Like many Americans, Romans ate rich food and drank way too much wine. Exercise was avoided whenever possible.

In contrast, the Israelites lived very naturally. They lived close to the earth and in accord with nature. While the Romans ate and drank themselves to death, the Israelites enjoyed far greater health by simply obeying God's plan for a healthy life. Consequently each culture would reap the benefits of their lifestyles.

The Israelites enjoyed an agriculture rich in all kinds of beans, lentils, millet, figs, dates, melons and so on. They recognized that their food was a gift from God, and they truly regarded their food as such.

They never took the time to make rich creams or sauces or gravies; they would add herbs to their nutrition-rich food. This would give the food zest to the taste.

Another important factor to consider is that the Israelites ate sparingly. Breakfast would be very small while lunch would consists of bread, vegetables and fruit. Dinner would be a stew with meat and vegetables. The members of the family would dip bread into the pot. It would be spiced with herbs and other local spices. Their diet would be high in fiber and low in fat.

Garlic and onions were believed to hold almost miraculous properties and were used freely in their food. We know today that they are capable of stimulating the immune system and slashing heart attack risk by preventing potentially fatal blood clots. Garlic and onions also act most effectively as antibiotics and were staples in their diet.

There have been some 2,600 plants identified as growing in the Holy Land, of which the Bible mentions at least 110 of them. Every one of them would be approved by health-conscious modern nutrition experts.[1]

Every culture that used herbs as medicines had a great respect for them. By in large they ate very naturally and lived very close to the earth.

As we study herbs, we will focus on those used primarily for medicinal purposes.

There are approximately 38,000 species of plants already identified on planet earth. But it is believed that there are several hundred thousand plants still to be discovered especially in the Amazon rainforest. These plants will have a potential for healing all kinds of diseases.

Out of the number of known plants there are approximately 260,000 that are classified as a higher species since they contain chlorophyll.[2] These plants perform a biological function known as photosynthesis. In photosynthesis, a plant utilizes the energy provided by the sun to manufacture carbohydrates from carbon dioxide and water. As a result, all plants have the potential to become medicines for all kinds of health needs. Plants take in the raw materials such as carbon dioxide, water and sunlight and convert them into beneficial nutrients. In addition to this oxygen is a by-product of the process.

The ancients did not know how herbs actually worked but they had great insights in using them medicinally.

Miracle Herbal Cures

Herbs are rich in compounds that are pharmacologically active, which can have a profound effect on various animal tissues and their organs. Herbs may be used as drugs in treating thousands of diseases. They have the power not only to cure disease but also to prevent disease.

The ancients understood that the leaves, roots, fruit, flowers, bark stems and even seeds could be used in the treatment of disease. Any of these parts could contain active ingredients that give the herb its medicinal properties.

Today we have an herbal pharmacy that truly is rich in every aspect. We have herbs that target specific organ systems and other herbs that may be used as general overall tonics. There are herbs that stimulate organ systems while others have a relaxing effect. There are herbs that will enhance the immune system while others kill bacteria.

HERBS: HOW MUCH IS TOO MUCH?

When herbs were first used by the ancients, they had no understanding of what the herbs actually contained. They simply understood that using certain herbs elicited specific results. Today we know from modern laboratory techniques how herbs actually work. Thus we are able to analyze the extracts from the herb itself. Yet there is so much needed work to be done on herbs.

Remember herbs are medicines and must be used with caution. Before trying herbs make sure you know what they do and their possible side effects. There are herbs that should not be mixed because of the possible adverse side effects. They must not be used indiscriminately. Always follow directions and never exceed the recommended dosage. There are few medical problems that will occur from taking herbal remedies, but there is the potential for an allergic or toxic reaction.

Approximately 1 percent of all plants are poisonous. A skilled botanist has no problem in selecting herbs, but to the untrained, herbs can pose real problems. It's best to buy herbs from a good health store, knowing that you're purchasing what you need without the risk of poison.

It is good to know that numerous companies are taking into consideration many of the concerns we have had toward processed herbs. Many companies that previously sold only vitamins and minerals now sell herbs. Rest assured they're producing quality products. Many refuse to use herbs that have been treated with pesticides and now question the means of processing them.

Herbs are sold in various packaged forms. Health food stores and herbalist shops will sell them in the following ways:

1. Capsules and tablets: It is now possible to purchase the more popular herbs in capsules and tablets. The dosage of the herb is dependent upon the strength of the herb itself. Some recommend taking two or three capsules daily, or more. However, make sure you follow the recommended dosage.

2. Extract or tinctures: Soaking them in an alcohol solution for a designated period of time produces these liquid herbal products. Most preparations will require 10 to 30 drops several times a day. It is imperative that pregnant women and children avoid these preparations. It is the same with diabetics.

3. Powders: Herbs in a powdered form usually are mixed with water or juice. Because most people like the convenience of taking capsules, empty capsules are now available, and you can put the powder in the capsules.

4. Dried herbs: Dried herbs are available in bulk form, usually found in large glass jars. Buying the herbs in bulk is less costly but does present a problem for storage. These should be stored in airtight containers and out of direct sunlight. Often times these herbs are used in making teas but may be placed in capsules.

5. Prepared teas: Multitudes of prepared teas are now on the market and are sold in bag form. If you buy your herbal teas in the health food store, please be aware that these are more potent than the ones you buy in the grocery store.

6. Juice: Herbs sold in juice form should be used according to the directions found on the bottle.

7. Combination herbal products: Today there is a very wide range of herbal remedies combining two or more herbs in capsule, tea and other forms such as extracts. Use these only as directed.

8. Creams and ointments: Today numerous herbs are used as external ointments and creams. Everything from skin care to fat reduction products are on the market but use only as directed. It is best to research some of the claims by a particular product before purchasing.

9. Essential oils: Oils can be used for baths, perfumes, massage oils and for the use of aromatherapy, which is the art of using certain fragrances to create health and relaxation. Oils are for external use only and must never be taken internally.

10. Personal hygiene: There are numerous products on the market that are totally natural, pure and without any synthetic ingredients. Herbal shampoos, facial cleansers, deodorants, moisturizers and toothpaste are only some of the numerous products now on the market. There are many new hypoallergenic cosmetic lines now available that are used with great results. Also, they have not been treated on animals that otherwise would have been a form of cruelty for the animals.

It is very important to purchase "fresh" dried herbs. In other words, try to purchase herbs in a good health food store where the herbs don't have a long shelf life. Do not use herbs where the expiration date already has transpired. An unopened bottle of capsules has a long shelf life. However, if they have been opened, it is best to throw them away after some time.

Let us understand that the amount of an herb that a person might need varies from individual to individual. Factors such as height, weight and age will determine the amount of the herb that is necessary. Heavier people require a larger dose than a thinner person does, and an older person requires less than a younger person. If the person taking herbs is sensitive to medications, it is logical to take smaller amounts. Please be advised that the daily amount of herbs to be taken will find flexibility in the amount of the dosage.

There is no need to take larger amount of herbs if the smaller dosage is beneficial. Be careful not to exceed the dosage recommended on the bottle. Remember, we are dealing with very powerful natural medicines. Again, it is necessary to know that certain herbs must not be taken over a period of a long time.

The best time to take herbs will be dependent upon your response to them. Some individuals become nauseous if they take them on an empty stomach. For them, it is best to take the herb right before eating or after meals.

Obviously, don't take an herb that causes stimulation prior to bedtime. Also, it would be foolish to take an herb that causes sleepiness just prior to going to work. Common sense must be used when taking any kind of herbal or natural medicine.

THE ANCIENT HERBALISTS

When I was a very young child, my grandfather would take me to the woods and show me various trees and plants from which he would make his herbal cures. Since he learned the art of herbalism from his mother, naturally, he never wrote any of these down on paper. Of course, she never wrote down any of her herbal cures and insights. He would sell his so-called "winter cures" for twenty-five cents. Amazingly, his medicines actually worked. Unfortunately, there was no written record of his cures as it was through the centuries.

Many herbalists today believe this wonderful art actually predates the human race. We know that animals seek out certain plants when they are ill. It is believed that early humans began watching their animals when they were sick and began to use the same plants when they became sick.

The very earliest "herbal guide" was found to be written by the Sumerians some five thousand years ago.[3] These ancient people used such herbs as caraway and thyme for their many ills. Many scholars feel that Ayurvedam, the traditional medicine of India, may even precede the Sumerians. We know that the Ancient Egyptians used onions and garlic as their most common cure for just about anything. These have been found written in hieroglyphics on papyrus dating back thousands of years.

The Chinese have always used herbs for healing. The "Wu Shi Er Bing Fang" or "Prescriptions for Fifty-two Diseases" dates back between 1065 B.C. and 711 B.C.[4] The Chinese used herbs known today as licorice, ginger and astragalus with great success. Again the Bible is full of herbs such as aloe, myrrh, and frankincense, which are used today with positive results.

Hippocrates (460-377 B.C.), who is considered "the father of modern-day medicine," lists between three hundred and four hundred plant cures in his many writings. Dioscorides, a Greek physician, lists five hundred plant remedies in his herbal book, *De Materia Medica,* which was written in the first century.[5] Galen (A.D.), a famous Roman physician who ministered to the Roman emperor and his gladiators, often used herbal cures in his medical practice.

During the Middle Ages, herbal healing was based upon ancient formulas that were passed from one generation to the next. The only problem was that there was no uniformed system of healing. So one herbalists might use a series of concoctions that another herbalists might totally

Miracle Herbal Cures

reject. Another problem was ignorance. The Roman Catholic Church emphasized faith healing but at the same time the monks would use various herbal remedies handed down from early Greek and Roman times. During the Middle Ages the monasteries abounded and many of them grew their own herbal gardens to treat themselves and their parishioners. When the printing press was finally invented, this gave the masses the ability to know about herbs and various healing modalities. A Tudor family physician, John Gerard, produced his first commentary, *The Herbal or General Historie of Plantes,* in 1597. [6]

At the same time there appeared another gentleman, Nicholas Culpeper, who wrote *The English Physician*. This interesting book is filled with folklore, astrology and botanical medicine. I was introduced to Culpeper's works while studying herbalism in England. Indeed Culpeper knew his herbs, but some of his strange involvement with astrology shouldn't be taken seriously. He had a special knowledge of herbs but was despised by the English medical establishment after the appearance of his book. Culpeper's book was a translation of the "Latin Pharmacopeia," which was unavailable to the general population. Unfortunately, Culpeper died at an early age while fighting on the Parliamentary side during the English Civil War and was wounded in the chest. Even to this day he is considered a folk hero by many in England.

When the English Puritans arrived in the New World, they brought with them their knowledge of herbalism as practiced in England. This was shared with the Native Americans who, in turn, showed them their vast array of herbs. Many Native American herbs and cures would eventually make their way to Europe.

During the 1800s, Western medicine turned to the chemical side of treatment. Herbs were discouraged from being used and the focus was chemical compounds as cures. Herbal medicine continued in the United States by numerous practitioners of medicine for some time. Eventually chemical treatments such as arsenic, sulphur and mercury found their way into all kinds of chemical preparations. Only homeopathic physicians continued using herbs and various non-chemical preparations in their practice.

Today we are seeing a resurgence of interest in herbs. When we realize that herbs are truly miraculous, this becomes a golden opportunity to our health. Natural things do not have the often dreaded side effects that chemical compounds so easily create.

Chapter Two

Using Herbs Wisely

Herbal healing is a wonderful but simple means of healing. For centuries it has been known as the "Art of Simpling." Herbs were called "simples" because a single herb could treat a multitude of maladies. Today, there is a danger of getting so caught-up with the encyclopedias of herbs that it will actually distract from what we truly need to know. It is best to know and be involved with a lesser number of herbs so that one might experience the joy of true "simpling."

There are three principles of simpling that, if known, will aid you immensely in your personal health and that of others.

Miracle Herbal Cures

THE ART OF SIMPLING

Principle One: Use herbs from your local area.

Usually the type of sickness that is contracted is somewhat dependent upon the local environment. Herbs that are grown in the local area will take on the distinctive characteristics of that environment. Herbs grown in your area are most useful for the treatment of conditions associated with the climate and other aspects of your locale. For instance, people in the northern United States contact more colds, flus and bronchitis than those living in the South. People in the south suffer from parasitic infections.

Principle Two: The use of mild herbs.

Mild herbs may be taken freely and will stimulate all the systems of the body. This in turn will create health and aid in fighting various afflictions. Consequently any mild herb that is grown in the area may be prepared for usage.

Principle Three: Mild herbs must be used in large amounts.

Inasmuch as the herb is mild, larger dosages are necessary to effect a cure.

There is a great difference in drinking]herbal tea for enjoyment and using the herbal tea for healing. If a small amount of the herb is used in a cup of boiling water, no cure will be evident. It will be necessary to drink a stronger tea over a period of several days to find a beneficial cure for the ailment.

In order for an herbal cure to be effective, the individual must remove those things from his diet

Using Herbs Wisely

that do not promote general good health. If the disease is caused by something in the person's lifestyle, that too must be eliminated. It is so necessary to eat good nutritional foods and take the needed supplements, not only to prevent a disease, but also to assist in the healing process.

When herbs are being used in an acute ailment, it takes only a few days to see improvement. Again, there must be a lifestyle change if that lifestyle is unhealthy. You can't eat all the wrong foods and expect herbs to miraculously heal you. Even after the acute ailment has been healed, it is best to continue using those herbs for two or three more weeks to insure a more complete healing and prevent the ailment from returning. If there isn't a healing within three weeks of taking the herbs, it is best to change the herbs. Find out exactly what herb is truly needed for your situation.

Herbs are excellent in treating a chronic condition. Usually several herbs are compounded together to create a balanced formula that can be taken in a tea form. This allows the individual to take a stronger tea of two or three cups per day. It is necessary to understand that these chronic diseases have taken much time to develop and it will require much patience over a period of time for the response that you desire. Usually, there needs to be a healing of emotions and changes in your thinking pattern. Most herbalists will tell you that for each year the chronic condition has existed, it will take a good month of herbal therapy for the eventual healing of that ailment.

Miracle Herbal Cures

Herbal Therapy

The body is a wonderful complex organism that does everything in cycles. Consequently, there will be needed breaks in herbal therapy. Fasting one day a week will give the body rest and allow it to respond more effectively when the herbal therapy is continued.

People who lack understanding of how herbs work will lack commitment to the program. Many people are very inconsistent because some dosages may be rather large. But there are times when larger dosages are needed to have a lasting effect. Most of all, people will have problems with herbal therapy because of improper diets. We cannot underestimate the need of a good diet.

It is best to know what an herb can actually do since herbs have various functions. Coordinating the herbs with the condition of the individual is vital since herbs can become dangerous and may cause more harm than good. The very first principle of modern medicine is to do no harm, and harm can come about if an herb is taken indiscriminately.

Herbs eliminate and detoxify the body. There are herbs used as laxatives, diuretics, diaphoretics and even blood purifiers. They also can be used to counteract physical symptoms. This then allows the body to begin to heal itself. There are herbs to help build the body and even tone it.

The initial stage of herbal treatment is for the purpose of elimination. This consists of removing the toxins from the body that can be the physical cause of the disease or even the result of the dis-

Using Herbs Wisely

ease. During this period there will be a depletion of energy and perhaps the person will feel even weaker. It is important not to give herbs of this nature to individuals who are already weak or suffering from a prolonged degenerative illness. Those with this type of illness need to build up prior to starting such an elimination program to regain strength and energy. At this point herbs should be given to maintain the body and to build it up. Once the condition has been stabilized, only then is it possible to proceed with the appropriate herbs for elimination and rejuvenation.

Those individuals whose diets are rich in animal products such as meat, cheese and milk need to eliminate the toxins and poisons from their bodies. For those who go to the opposite extreme by eating only vegetables and fruits, they will need to have a cleansing herb to help them regain their strength. Those individuals usually suffer from the problem of poor assimilation. Usually they respond well by being treated with the roots and barks of trees made into a herbal tea.

Herbs can be truly miraculous when conventional medicine has failed. After surgeries, radiation and chemotherapy it is good to know that God created herbs to help restore those who have suffered through the modalities of man. Herbs can do so much when they are properly used. Often times when herbs have been used in accordance with their designated purpose, surgery, radiation and chemotherapy may not be at all necessary.

Miracle Herbal Cures

WAYS HERBS ARE USED

When using herbs we need to be aware of the various methods or ways they might be utilized. There are eight different ways in which herbs may be used when treating ailments in the body.

1. Stimulation

Stimulation is accomplished by throwing off the illness, bringing the body back to where it belongs. Herbal stimulates, when combined with other herbs, do promote the elimination, maintaining and building of the body. There are numerous effective stimulants such as ginger, cayenne, garlic, black pepper and cloves.[1]

Stimulates function to increase the metabolism, encourage better circulation and break up obstruction in the bloodstream. Since they increase the warmth of the human body, consequently, the body's own recuperative powers will be strengthened to throw off the disease. Stimulates can increase the vitality of the body that might have been lost through chronic illness.

Illnesses characterized by reduced energy and that slow feeling are successfully treated by stimulate therapy. Flus, colds and sinus conditions often respond very well to stimulation.

When there is a digestion problem, stimulants are beneficial. These aromatic herbs stimulate the action of both the stomach and small intestine.

It's important to note that we are not talking about coffee or black tea as stimulants. The problem with coffee is that it has an acidic effect, which creates a toxic condition in the blood and digestive tract. It is important not to confuse these stimulants with beneficial herbs that function primarily as stimulants. Coffee and black tea have detrimental effects on the body and eventually create other health problems.

Stimulation therapy should not be used if there has been a prolonged disease since the body's strength reserve has already been depleted.

2. Tranquilization

Tranquilization therapy is used when the individual is experiencing great unrest and stress. There are three different kinds of herbs that bring tranquilization to the human body: demulcents, nervine and antispasmodics. These may be used intensely over a short period of time. Two or three days are recommended with an hourly dosage if necessary.

Demulcent herbs function to lubricate the joints, bones and gastrointestinal tract. They even have a quieting effect upon our stressful lifestyles.

Nervines have been known to feed the nervous system and help create a balanced energy level. Good examples of nervines include skullcap, catnip, wood betony, lady's slipper and valerian.[2]

Antispasmodics have the propensity to calm the nervous tension in muscles. This would not only include the muscles of the skeleton but also the smooth muscles of internal organs. They help reduce pain due to tension. Good examples of antispasmodics include lobelia, valerian, kava kava, black cohosh and dong quai.[3]

The need for adequate calcium in the diet cannot be overestimated. Calcium benefits the function of the nervous system and all muscles. The heart is directly affected by a lack of sufficient calcium. Calcium brings great peace to the human body when the mineral levels are in proper proportion.

3. Blood Purification

In general, most herbalists agree that if the blood is cleansed all diseases will eventually decrease. Blood purifiers play a very important role in herbal therapies.

The blood and lymph of the body must be periodically cleansed since they carry a variety of toxic substances, most of which are acidic. These toxic substances are usually absorbed into the body from the food we eat. Chemical preservatives being used today in our food are so numerous that it only benefits us to cleanse the blood periodically. Add to this the natural wastes created by the body itself and it is easy to see the necessity of blood purification.

The organs of the body most responsible for blood purification are the small intestine, liver, kidneys and colon. The small intestine separates all different kinds of useful nutrients from those that are not beneficial at all. All the other organs are considered secondary organs of the body in this process.

One of the best known herbs used for blood purification is echinacea angustifolia, otherwise known as "prairie doctor" or "kansas snakeroot." Other excellent herbal blood purifiers may include: burdock root, dandelion, red clover, sarsaparilla, sassafras and Oregon grape root.[4]

Using Herbs Wisely

Blood purifiers play a most important role in the treatment of infections. The herbs help reduce toxins found in the blood system. These herbs will help stimulate the natural defense mechanism of the body to fight the invading bacterial or virus by reducing the amount of heat from the infection and even help remove the moisture found in the infected area. Echinacea also promotes the production of white blood cells needed to destroy the invading enemy.

4. Tonicfication

Tonics are used to build up the strength of the body's various systems. Tonics are recommended for those whose vital energy has been depleted. Tonic therapy may be used not only for acute illnesses, but even for chronic illnesses. Tonics also can be used to maintain good health.

Tonics are most beneficial for all organs of the body. They provide necessary vitamins and minerals that the body needs for good health. Alfalfa, comfrey and dandelion leaves are very good tonics. These are most inexpensive, but have almost miraculous properties about them.

Tonic herbs assist in the elimination of various deficiencies. It should be noted that if the body is deficient in one area, other organs are indirectly affected by that deficiency.

The Chinese are very advanced in tonic therapy. They are successful in treating chronic diseases and they use tonics for disease prevention. This is a concept we are just beginning to learn.

5. Diuresis

Diuresis deals with the control of bodily fluids, which consists mostly of water. As we learn the art of balancing the fluid levels in our bodies, we are then able to restore and maintain continued good health.

Fluid levels in the body fluctuate very rapidly, and emotions are directly linked to body fluid levels. Just prior to the menstrual cycle, women often complain of water retention. When the body has too much water, this can lead to feelings of weakness, paranoia and even depression.[5] When there is too little water in the body, it is not unusual for a fit of anger to flare up. We do know that it is unwise to drink too much water or other liquids when having meals because liquids greatly affect the digestive juices.

We are able to reduce the amount of water within the body by using a variety of diuretic herbs. Some excellent diuretic herbs include: prince's pine, buchu leaves, horsetail, cleavers, corn silk, uva ursi leaves and juniper berries.[6] These herbs increase the flow of urine, decrease the blood pressure and cleanse the bloodstream.

In order to have a good balance of water in the body, it becomes necessary to regulate the intake amount. Remember that our foods do have water within them. A good sign that there is too much water in the body is by checking the bags or darkness under the eyes. This is an indication that the kidneys are waterlogged. Check not only on the amount of water taken in, but also the other liquids you might be drinking.

Using Herbs Wisely

6. Sweating

Cold, flu and even fever respond readily to sweating. Stimulating herbs are the best because they will increase the circulation and promote a good sweat. Important stimulating diaphoretics include teas made from elder flower and peppermint, bonset, cayenne, ginger, lemon and honey. These should be taken as hot teas. The sweating effect will begin almost immediately. These very same teas, when taken as cold teas, will have a diuretic effect. Taking a very hot bath prior to drinking the teas will aid the effect of sweating. After a hot bath, it is good to go to bed with a very warm blanket wrapped around the body to induce further sweating.

7. Emesis

Emesis means vomiting or ridding the stomach of all of its contents. This may be necessary if one has been accidentally poisoned. Again, if there is a bad combination of foods with the resultant effect of a sick stomach, vomiting may be induced.

There are several good herbal products that will induce vomiting. Ipecac is an excellent herbal syrup found at almost any good drug store. Ipecac will cause vomiting within a few seconds. Lobelia maybe used in the tincture form. For best results, this must be taken three times within a half-hour period.

8. Purging

This is cleansing the colon due to toxic waste, excess secretions or constipation. Constipation is the result of a poor diet and lack of exercise and is a serious problem in today's Western society.

Miracle Herbal Cures

Purging should not be administered to an individual who is very weak or has abdominal pain. Pain in the abdomen may be directly related to the appendix. If purging should take place, there is the possibility of the appendix rupturing, a condition that only surgery can correct.

Herbs such as cascara sagrada ark and rhubarb root have a laxative action by stimulating the secretion of the bile into the small intestine. This increases the peristalsis, the natural rhythmic contractions of the intestines, moving the feces along the route of elimination. Licorice and slippery elm are more mild and may be used by adults and children.

Aloe vera works very well since it creates peristaltic action and may help those with more advanced illnesses without the fear of harming the individual. Psyllium seed, flaxseeds and chia seeds will swell up with water forcing the movement of the feces.

As we will observe in the following chapters, when we use herbs wisely they can produce miraculous results in many of our organs and body parts.

It is now possible to purchase a combination of these herbs at your local health food store in either pill or capsule form. Truly they will do the job!

Chapter Three

Strengthening the Heart

Do you have heart problems? If you do, you need to become acquainted with several outstanding herbs that will definitely help you become well.

For centuries the Christian church has regarded "hawthorn" *(Crataegus oxycantha)* as being sacred. It is believed that the crown of thorns that was placed on Christ's head was made of hawthorn. Even today, there is a grove of hawthorn trees that still stands outside of Jerusalem on the Mount of Olives.

Hawthorn has numerous benefits; it can help and even prevent certain heart conditions and diseases. It has the ability to assist the heart in better utilization of the oxygen that it receives. It functions as a mild dilator of coronary vessels and serves as a peripheral vasodilator (dilating the blood vessels away from the heart). This in turn lowers the blood pressure and reduces the burden placed on the heart itself.[1]

Studies have shown that hawthorn is excellent as a tonic and considered valuable for improvement of cardiac weakness, angina pectoris, valve murmurs from the heart, valve defects, an enlarged heart, sighing respiration and nerve depression of unexplained chronic fatigue.[2] There is new evidence that hawthorn is effective in facilitating mitral regurgitation, easing cardiac pain and regulating rapid or feeble heart beat. In addition to this, hawthorn is excellent in helping with difficulty in breathing due to ineffective heart action and the lack of oxygen in the blood. Many athletes say that hawthorn helps the heart when there has been over-exertion. It is most helpful in reducing cholesterol levels. It encourages the good cholesterol, HDL, and helps lower the bad cholesterol, LDL.

Scientists now know that hawthorn increases coronary blood flow and improves myocardial metabolism, allowing the heart to function at a greater capacity with less oxygen.

This wonderful herb acts to lower blood pressure by dilating the blood vessels thus allowing the blood to flow more freely. It will act directly on the heart muscle to help a damaged heart work more effectively. Recent studies have shown that the principle ingredients, which are flavonoids, help dilate the blood vessels and produce some reduction in blood pressure.

We also know that hawthorn is very effective in relieving restlessness and insomnia. If hawthorn is used on a regular basis, it will help prevent heart disease.

DIGITALIS
(DIGITALIS PURPUREA)

The discovery of this beautiful but deadly herb came about in an incredible way. In 1775, English physician William Withering discovered digitalis, which is also called foxglove. He had heard about an amazing old woman, a witch, who lived in Shropshire, England, who had a profound knowledge of herbs. At that time, Withering was treating a patient with congestive heart failure who was not expected to live.

Withering consulted the old woman who gave him a curious mixture consisting of a dozen or more herbs and wanted her payment. Withering thought her price was way too high. She told him to either pay the price or suffer the consequences of a spell; he decided to pay her the price.

After making a tea out of the mixture of herbs, he administered this tea to his patient every two to four hours. After five days of treatment his patient was out of bed and walking, showing enormous improvement.

Withering analyzed the remaining mixture of herbs and realized that foxglove was the main ingredient.[3] This became an outstanding medication and is still used to this day to treat heart disease.

For over 220 years, doctors are still using this powerful drug to treat congestive heart failure. It also is used in treating atherosclerosis and hypertension, which are related to heart disease. This drug helps increase the contractibility and improves the tone of the heart muscle itself. Consequently a much stronger heartbeat is produced. We know that digitalis slows the wildly beating ventricles to a normal level by blocking or delaying the conduction of the electric impulse through the atrioventricular node.[4] This herb does increase the heart stroke, which then doubles or even triples the amount of blood being oxygenated by the lungs. Due to the heart improvement, the kidneys are directly affected and the output is increased.

Digitalis is very potent. It can be a great blessing by improving the heart functioning or it can be a curse. Too much of this good thing can kill you. A physician who knows how to administer this drug must regulate it.

OTHER HEART-HEALTHY HERBS

Let us not forget the everyday onion. It is one of the oldest and most versatile remedies known to mankind. It can be used to treat the common cold by making a syrup: mixing one onion with honey. This will relieve congestion and coughing. My grandfather made a cough syrup every winter to help his children get over their colds and flus.

An onion a day is not only good for overall health, but it also can help the heart. Studies now show that eating a medium-size onion a day will lower the overall cholesterol. It raises the HDL and lowers LDL. Onions will lower blood pressure and help prevent blood clotting. The National Cancer

Strengthening the Heart

Institute has stated that people who eat foods high in allium vegetables, such as onion and garlic, experience less stomach and colon cancer. Many cultures believe that eating onions will help restore sexual potency.

There is an ancient Chinese herb known as "fo-ti" *(polygonum multiforum)* that is used primarily as a rejuvenating tonic. In China this herb is called "ho shou wu." The Chinese believe that this herb can even prevent gray hair. The Chinese have shown us that fo-ti can prevent premature aging. It also is believed to increase fertility, strength and vigor. Tests have shown that it has an antitumor propensity.

It is also known for its ability to prevent heart disease and lower blood pressure. It even reduces the danger of blood clotting.[5]

We must not forget the great benefits of eating garlic. Garlic *(allium sativum)* has been used for centuries to treat heart disease and high blood pressure. This amazing herb has been used with much success to treat infections and tuberculosis.

Because of a shortage of medicine, Dr. Albert Schweitzer, a missionary in Africa during the 1950s, used garlic to treat cholera, typhus and amebic dysentery.

The Russians have used garlic extensively on the battlefields during World War I and II. Because of a shortage of antibiotics, the Russians used garlic as if it were penicillin.

Garlic also is used as a anticoagulant to diminish the effects of blood clots. It is known to lower cholesterol, creating a higher level of HDL. It lowers blood pressure and at the same time it helps lower the level of LDL.

Miracle Herbal Cures

It is now known that garlic has a toxic effect on some tumor cells. The National Cancer Institute is conducting research on garlic for its cancer-inhibiting abilities. Studies have shown that people in India and China who eat garlic as a staple in their diets have less cancer and heart disease. Garlic is even good for digestion. However, women who are breast-feeding should not eat garlic because the toxic is passed onto the infant from the mother's milk.

It has been known for centuries that garlic oil can relieve earaches and even help heal some skin disorders. A word of caution: do not to eat more than ten garlic cloves per day as they can become very toxic. As with all good things, moderation is needed.

Evening primrose oil is well known to reduce cholesterol. There was a study done by Efamol Research Institute in Canada in 1983 concerning the use of primrose oil for cholesterol reduction. After a period of three months there was an average drop of 30 percent of cholesterol levels. Evening primrose oil also is know to lower blood pressure.[6]

Chinese herbalists have known for centuries that ginseng is an excellent heart tonic. Ginseng aids in lowering cholesterol, lowering blood sugar and helps normalize blood pressure.

Cayenne pepper is most beneficial in lowering triglycerides and LDLs. Women with an elevated triglyceride level over 190 milligrams are in danger of developing heart disease; a little cayenne pepper in cooking can be beneficial to them.

People living in Mediterranean countries have much less heart disease than Europeans or even

Strengthening the Heart

Americans. It is most likely due to the fact that they use olive oil for cooking and as a salad oil. Olive oil is a monounsaturated fat that lowers overall blood cholesterol. It does not reduce the benefits of the HDL cholesterol. HDL is the good cholesterol that we need to have in a much higher proportion than the LDL cholesterol.

Recent studies show that the husks of the psyllium plant can lower blood cholesterol levels in men with moderately high levels of cholesterol. Certainly if this can help men, it can do the same for women. This is an herb that must be used with caution since there are those who are allergic to it.

Even good old-fashioned oat bran can aid in cholesterol reduction. Oat bran is a water-soluble form of fiber that is very rich in beta glucan. Eating about two ounces of this daily will certainly reduce cholesterol nicely.

If you have heart disease it is necessary to know about the benefits of Coenzyme Q_{10}. This miracle worker is not an herb but an enzyme with remarkable healing powers. It is found in every cell of the body and is absolutely necessary for life. At one time it was called ubiquinone. Coenzyme Q_{10} is quinone, a cyclic organic compound essential to sustain life itself.

This glorious product is a vital link in the mitachondrila chain supplying biochemicals needed for cellular energy. It also helps to create a more efficient use of oxygen in the body. It is known to reduce free radical damage since it is a very potent antioxidant and it lowers the risk of periodontal disease. It aids in increasing energy levels, which most of us wish we had more of. What it does best of all is enhance the pumping action of the heart and boost the immune system.

There is a definite relationship between vitamin E and CoQ_{10}. Beware that it is fragile and easily destroyed by oxidation and processing. Cooking also destroys this precious enzyme.

CoQ_{10} is helpful in the treatment of chronic fatigue, the prevention and control of periodontal disease, cancer and AIDS. It helps to reduce high blood pressure, but does not affect normal blood pressure levels.

There is an old French medicine for the heart. The famous herbalist, Maurice Messegue, recommends mullein for palpitation, irregular heartbeat, angina and other coronary diseases. He recommends taking two handfuls of coarsely cut leaves and flowers and cooking them in $1^1/_2$ quarts of boiling water for an hour until about a pint of this remains. Then strain and add 3 tablespoons of blackstrap molasses and $^1/_2$ teaspoon of glycerin to give it a long shelf life. He recommends taking 1 tablespoon of this syrup twice daily in between meals. Morning and evening are the best times to take this preparation. If pressure builds up in the heart, he recommends taking more of the mixture.[7]

These are only a few of the many herbal cures available for the heart. They do work and should be used with caution. Experts don't promise a miracle from using these herbs but they certainly predict wondrous results.

Chapter Four

High Blood Pressure and Blood Cleansing

It is common knowledge that one of the main causes of high blood pressure is stress. There has never been such a time as now when people are under unusual stress. There are stress management classes and seminars to help people better understand stress and how to overcome it. We need to identify those things in our lives that are causing the stress and remove them if possible.

If you're going to reduce stress in your life, you need to discern and know what circumstances cause you to react to the things people say and do. What is it that makes people push your buttons? When you recognize the stress in your life, then you can do something about it. Only you have the ability to change your situation. What you think or

Miracle Herbal Cures

feel about something is *your choice.* You can change your life if you truly want it to change.

There are several lifestyle factors that negatively influence high blood pressure. Among them are the three S's: salt, smoking and stress. Drinking coffee, drinking alcohol, eating a high fat diet, not getting enough daily exercise and having excess weight all contribute to high blood pressure.

Many drugs on the market today are very good in lowering blood pressure, but have side effects. Eating two to three servings a day of fresh fruits and deep green vegetables—including potassium-rich bananas, oranges, dried peas, and beans—will definitely get you on the road to lowering your blood pressure. Eating brown rice can help restore the vitality of blood vessels.

There are numerous good herbal cures for high blood pressure. Both garlic and cayenne have proven themselves to be two of the most effective herbs known to mankind in reducing blood pressure. Garlic is known as nature's blood thinner par excellence. The chemical structure of garlic prevents deadly clots from forming and promotes good blood circulation. It is excellent in reducing blood pressure and at the same time reduces cholesterol levels. There is no medication known today that can match the stunning versatility of this simple herb. It is understood that two chemicals, allicin and ajoene, are responsible for the most beneficial effects on the cardiovascular system.[1]

Another excellent herb, ginkgo, also improves blood flow to vital areas such as the heart and brain. Ginkgo blocks a substance called platelet activation factor (PAF), and if not checked this can cause internal blood clots that can eventually lead to heart attacks and strokes.

Studies now show that ginkgo can improve blood flow not only to the brain, but also to the extremities. For example, ginkgo is very beneficial for men who are experiencing problems with impotency. The blood flow to the penis is enhanced, causing greater erections.

Even after a stroke, ginkgo can help improve blood flow to the brain because it helps in speeding recovery. In the same manner, ginkgo improves blood flow to the heart and can possibly reduce the risk of heart attack by dissolving or preventing the nasty blood clots that cause them. This wonderful herb may be purchased in commercial preparations. Just follow the directions on the package and take it on a regular daily basis for best results.

We know from previous studies that hawthorne berries have healing properties for the heart. Hawthorne berries should be taken when one is attempting to reduce high blood pressure. These berries will strengthen the heart causing a greater regularity of the pumping action.

Vitamin B_6 combined with potassium will assist in reducing the water content of the body. By reducing the water content you reduce the pressure placed on the cardiovascular system. If there is persistent swelling, see a cardiologist. Swelling may be in the ankles, hands or face. Since each individual is different, it is important to stay in tune to and know how your body is functioning. Each body will react differently to water retention.

The good old-fashioned herb, valerian root, is a natural and harmless way to calm nerves and aid in blood pressure reduction. It is also known to reduce pain. Hops is another herb effective in calming the nervous system.

Calcium is known as the heart mineral since it has great calming effects and benefits to the heart. Be advised that the heart is a major consumer of calcium.

Let us not forget the essential amino acid L-Taurine that plays a major role in heart and nerve functions. L-Taurine is so very necessary in cholesterol metabolism. All of these herbs and minerals help the heart recover and even prevent heart attacks.

The blood of the human body must never be taken for granted. Most good herbalists consider blood as the very life fluid of the body. It is so necessary to keep your blood free of all toxins and poisons because your blood affects every cell in the body. If the blood is not pure, the body will suffer needlessly. Poisons and toxins can seep into the cells setting up the person for some major diseases along the way. A bacterial infection or any type of toxic material in the blood will adversely affect every part of the human body.

When the body is healthy, it is totally capable of detoxifying its own blood. Now let us look at several herbs and vegetables that can aid in blood cleansing.

OTHER HEART-HEALTHY HERBS

Red clover *(trifolium pratense)* is a most valued herb for its properties of blood cleansing. It has the ability to restore the alkaline balance of the body

High Blood Pressure and Blood Cleansing

and boost fertility in women.[2] Red clover also is rich in trace minerals necessary in many enzyme transactions within the body. This herb gained notoriety when herbalist Jason Winters used it along with the chaparral herb and others in an attempt to cure certain cancers.

Burdock *(arctium lappa)* has historic reputation of being a good blood cleanser. For hundreds of years herbalists have considered this herb to be a good source of nutrients to help build the body. My grandfather, George Washington McCann, called plants such as dandelion and burdock "great blood purifiers." Menomini and Micmac Indians were known to use this herb for skin sores. Cherokee Indians used it on a much broader range of ailments.

Burdock is excellent during pregnancy since it is filled with minerals that assist the hormones in balancing all systems. In addition, it will prevent water retention and jaundice.[3] It has been known for centuries as a strong liver purifier and hormone balancing herb with great value for the skin and also arthritic and glandular problems.

Burdock is especially good for blood cleansing since it eliminates long-term impurities from the blood very rapidly. It has been used as an antidote for acute poisoning. Burdock reduces swelling especially around the joints by improving kidney functioning. As a result of this, urine is increased in flowing out of the body. It aids in reducing harmful acids due to calcification deposits in the body.

Burdock has been used in the past as a poultice on certain forms of skin cancer. It is considered the most important herb for effectively treating skin problems such as blemishes, eczema, acne, psoriasis, boils and sties. In Europe during the past few centuries, burdock has been used as a remedy for patients with a prolapsed or displaced uterus.[4]

Chaparral *(larrea tridentata, L. divaricata)* is a nickname for "Creosote bush," which derives its name from the oil that is used to treat wood products. The word *Chaparral* comes from a Spanish word that means a "low growing shrub."

The Indians of Mexico have used this herb for centuries as an anti-cancer remedy. Numerous North American Indian tribes used chaparral for ailments relating to bacterial infections and proper bowel elimination.

Several universities in the United States have tested chaparral and found it to aid in dissolving various tumors and as another weapon in fighting cancer.

We now know that it is a strong antioxidant, pain killer and can even be used as an antiseptic. This herb works by constraining undesired cellular growth by using the respiratory process, which is present through the entire human system. Chaparral has for its basic constituent, NDGA (nordihydrogqaiaretic acid), a most powerful antioxidant and anti-tumor inhibitor, but this must be used only under a physician's direction.[5]

After 2,000 years of recorded history and the known benefits of this excellent herb, the FDA now desires to take this herb off the market. There are no known cases of abuse from the use of this God-given plant.

Echinacea *(Echinacea purpurea)* has been called the "king of the blood purifiers." This amazing herb improves lymphatic filtration and drainage. Some men have found it effective in treating an enlarged prostate gland and even weakness of the same gland.[6]

Science has now proven echinacea most useful in strengthening the immune system. The polysaccharides, fatty acids and glycosides in echinacea not only strengthen the immune system, but also give a feeling of overall general good health.

Naturopathics use echinacea often because it is a natural antibiotic and is an alternative to man made antibiotics. Echinacea is most beneficial for the treatment of toxic headaches coupled with vertigo. The relief that is given is truly outstanding. When there is a confused mental state caused by toxins, echinacea again has proven itself very helpful in relieving such a mental condition.

We know that Echinacea is an excellent blood cleanser. It works like penicillin in the human body with no known side effects. It is very good in expelling poisons and toxins from the body.

Yellow Dock *(Rumex crispus)* must not be left out of our list of wondrous herbs that cleanse the body. For centuries this herb has been known to cleanse the blood and build up the body by increasing the ability of the liver and other related organs to strain out impurities from the blood and lymph system. It has tonic properties that function as astringents purifying the blood supply to the glands.[7]

The roots of Yellow Dock contain a very high level of iron, which is so needed when anemia occurs during pregnancy or for anemia in general. It is excellent for the treatment of skin disease such

Miracle Herbal Cures

as infections or small growths. It helps reduce liver inflammation and gallbladder problems. When used sufficiently it acts as a laxative because it stimulates the flow of liver bile.

Yellow Dock is most effective in treating bleeding hemorrhoids. It also functions to create strength and endurance. In addition to this, Yellow Dock aids in the chemical balance of the body since it is high in mineral content.

It is so glorious to know that God has given us herbs for the healing of our bodies. At the same time we must make some changes in our diets if we are to remain healthy. All of us need to increase our intake of garlic, onions, celery, cucumbers, beets, carrots and parsley. Try using more sprouts in your diet since they are full of chlorophyll, which is so needed for detoxification. If possible, stay away from fast food restaurants. Try not to eat fried foods and those cooked in hydrogenated fats and oils. These will clog your arteries and veins and eventually there will be a price to pay.

Note of caution: Anyone who thinks he or she may have any sort of heart problem or abnormal blood pressure should consult a physician at once. The above herbal aids should be used only after approval by your health professional. This should not be a guessing game. Be wise and take your health seriously.

Chapter Five

God's Little Liver Pills

The liver is the largest and one of the most important internal organs within the human body. It functions as the body's chemical factory and regulates the levels of most other main chemicals in the bloodstream. It weighs about 2.5 to 3.3 pounds and is roughly a cone-shaped, reddish-brown organ that occupies the upper-right abdominal cavity.[1]

The liver, which has two main lobes, lies just beneath the diaphragm. It receives oxygenated blood from the hepatic artery and nutrient rich blood via the portal vein. The liver secretes bile, a fluid that leaves the liver through a network of ducts known as the bile ducts.[2] Within the liver itself, the small bile ducts and branches of the hepatic artery and the portal vein form what is known as a conduit system. This is referred to as the portal tracts.[3]

The liver produces important proteins that play a part in the immune system's defenses against infection. The liver also produces proteins for blood plasma, including albumin, which regulates the exchange of water between blood and tissues. When a blood vessel wall is damaged, the liver aids in blood coagulation. Another protein called globin, is a constituent of the oxygen-carrying pigment hemoglobin.

A main function of the liver is to store up glucose that is not required immediately by the body's cells. This will then be stored as glycogen. When the body is in need of more energy and heat, the liver converts the glycogen back to glucose and releases it into the bloodstream. This is all done under the direction of special hormones.

This marvelous organ regulates the blood level of amino acids, which are chemicals that form the building blocks of proteins. After eating a heavy meal, the liver will convert some of the amino acids into glucose, some into proteins, and some into urea that is passed on to the kidneys for excretion in the urine.[4]

With the aid of the kidneys, the liver acts to clear the blood of drugs and poisonous substances that would otherwise accumulate in the bloodstream, causing poor health. The liver absorbs the substances to be removed from the blood. It alters the chemical structure of the substances and even makes them water soluble. They are then excreted into the bile. Liver bile carries waste products away from the liver, which is then further carried out by the small intestine.

Although the liver is extremely complex in its functioning, it still is a remarkable and resilient organ. Up to three-quarters of its cells can be destroyed before it will stop functioning.

Fried, greasy foods and alcoholic beverages create fatty deposits. This "super sludge" can damage to the liver. When the liver becomes "gummed," it loses its ability to perform properly. The liver becomes very seriously compromised. Liver bile is vital in the breakdown and absorption of fats.

There are many wonderful herbs that aid the liver. We will cover only a few: Milk Thistle, dandelion, chaparral, stillingia and lecithin.

MILK THISTLE

Milk Thistle *(Silybum marianum)* has been used for hundreds of years with great success in treating liver disorders. It has been observed that the use of Milk Thistle extract has produced profound reversals of symptoms. This marvelous herb has been used to treat viral hepatitis and cirrhosis with much success.

Not only does this herb protect the liver, but it helps to rejuvenate it. It is known to protect the kidney, brain and other tissues from chemical toxins. Milk Thistle is most beneficial for the liver since it helps detoxify it from chemical toxins. This herb has been helpful in alcohol-induced fatty liver disorders, chronic hepatitis and chemically-induced fatty liver disorders.

The active ingredient in Milk Thistle is silymarin. This chemical helps increase protein synthesis in liver cells. It increases the activity of ribosomal RNA.[5] Silymarin will induce an alteration of liver cellular membranes and will help stop the absorption of many toxins.

Milk Thistle is known as a powerful free radical scavenger. This herb contains some of the most potent life-giving substances known to mankind. In addition to this, Milk Thistle has been found to maintain the basic function of the liver. Consequently, it helps clean the blood system, which has an overall effect of maintaining health and well being to the entire human body. It aids in blocking allergic and inflammatory reactions.

It is known to aid the immune system by increasing the production of T-lymphocytes and soluble proteins.[6] This is a very beneficial herb we find in God's natural medicine chest. Use it wisely and the results will be most pleasing.

DANDELION

Dandelion *(Taraxacum officinale)* is a potassium-rich herb. It is a tremendous natural diuretic that can help support the body's potassium levels, which might otherwise be depleted by the numerous pharmaceutical preparations used in treating water retention. Dandelion aids in detoxification, improving health and increasing joint mobility.

It is well established that dandelion will increase the flow of liver bile. It is so effective that the early stages of cirrhosis of the liver can be alleviated by consistent use.[7]

Dandelion is most effective in conditions where there is water retention due to heart problems. Again, its effectiveness is seen in cases of congestive jaundice. It is most excellent as a general tonic and perhaps the most widely used herb as a diuretic and liver tonic. Dandelion is very good when used in a salad.

Herbalists in Europe use the juice of the Dandelion root to treat diabetes, liver diseases and anemia.[8] It is considered to be the absolute best for such conditions as anemia because of its mineral content. It is estimated that dandelion greens contain 7,000 units of vitamin A; this will even cause a carrot to stand up and take notice! It is now known that whenever cancer is found, there is a vitamin.

Because dandelion acts as a diuretic, it will cause a greater flow of urine. It also will act as a natural, gentle laxative. It is most invigorating and strengthening for the entire body. This remarkable herb contains all the nutritive salts that are required for the body to cleanse the blood. It has the propensity to harden the enamel of the teeth.

The Chinese use the seeds as a strong antibiotic especially for sinus and lung infections. They also use dandelion to treat breast cancer.

CHAPARRAL

Inasmuch as we have already spoken about chaparral *(Larrea tridentata, L. Divaricata)*, we will briefly mention that this amazing herb is most advantageous for the liver.

Chaparral tones the body, rebuilds tissues and is very effective as a healer of the urethral tract, blood, liver and lymphatic system. It is very effective in cleansing the kidneys, so it is advisable to drink a lot of water with this herb.

Chaparral is a herb that helps cleanse and heal certain kinds of liver diseases and disorders.

STILLINGIA

Stillingia *(Stillingia sylvatica)* is a plant found in North America and is still in the throws of discovery. According to many herbalists, it has been an excellent antidote for syphilis. It is effective in the treatment of certain kinds of cancers and found beneficial in treating tuberculosis. This herb is a distinguished glandular stimulant and is of great benefit in the treatment of cystic fibrosis.

Stillingia is most effective in ridding the liver of toxic chemicals used in various cancer therapies. This herb must be used with caution and does best when it is combined with other herbs. As a liver cleanser, it must be used with caution due to side effects.

LECITHIN

Lecithin is a wonderful fatty substance that is greatly needed for both liver and gallbladder diseases. Lecithin is found in animal- and plant-based foods including liver, eggs, soybeans, peanuts and wheat germ.

Lecithin is an excellent source of the B vitamin, choline, primarily in the form called phosphatidylcholine. When this is in the body it rapidly breaks down into choline. Eating foods with lecithin will

Chapter Six

Osteoporosis: The Case of the Shrinking Human

Osteoporosis is a disease where the loss of protein matrix tissue from the bone takes place. As a result, the increased porosity of the bones causes them to become brittle and easily fractured.

Many physicians do not discriminate between osteoporosis and osteomalacia. While osteomalacia is considered the adult form of rickets, osteoporosis is most common among elderly people. Doctors diagnose any decrease in the density (thinning) of the bone as osteoporosis. In actual fact, decreased density may be caused by osteomalacia or by osteomalacia with osteoporosis.[1]

Western medicine considers osteoporosis as a natural part of aging. It is believed that by the age of 70, the density of the skeleton will be diminished as much as one third. Women, far more than men, seem to suffer from this disease due to hormonal influences. For unknown reasons, osteoporosis is far more common among whites than blacks.

Bone density naturally becomes thinner as a person ages, but women seem to be far more vulnerable to osteoporosis after menopause since their ovaries no longer produce estrogen, which is known to help maintain bone mass.

The most common causes of osteoporosis include the removal of the ovaries and a diet deficient in calcium, an essential mineral for good bone health. In addition, certain hormonal disorders, such as Cushing's syndrome, prolonged treatment with corticosteroid drugs, and lack of exercise can cause osteoporosis.

Studies indicate that smokers and drinkers suffer far more from this disease than non-smokers and non-drinkers. For some unknown reason this disease is associated with chronic obstructive lung disorders, such as bronchitis and emphysema.[2]

There are several herbs and minerals that can minimize the disease and, in some cases, totally prevent it. Herbs such as Alfalfa and Horsetail Grass play an important role in its prevention.

ALFALFA

Alfalfa *(Medicago sativa)* is a member of the legume family. English herbalist John Gerard writes of it as early as 1597 and recommended it for upset stomachs. It is now known that the leaves of the plant actually contain eight essential amino acids.

In Latin America, Colombian Indians have used Alfalfa for coughs while the Costanoan Indians

Osteoporosis: The Case of the Shrinking Human

apply it as a poultice for earaches.[3] The Chinese use Alfalfa for treating intestinal and kidney disorders.

In the Middle East, Alfalfa is known as the "father of all herbs." The origin of the word comes from a Persian word *asparti* meaning "horse fodder." This wonderful herb has been cultivated for hundreds of years and probably originated somewhere in Armenia.

The Spanish brought Alfalfa from Europe as they were civilizing the New World. Gold prospectors brought it to California. European colonists religious freedom introduced the herb in the eastern and central United States.

Alfalfa is full of vitamin C and is a much better source than even citrus fruits. It is also full of vitamin K, which is so needed by pregnant women who experience morning sickness. It is an excellent source of beta-carotene, necessary for a healthy immune system. It is full of vitamin E and has the highest source of calcium than any other herb. It is excellent in treating osteoporosis since the high calcium level is easily absorbed in the human body.

There is a problem for human beings who try eating this plant. Unlike animals, our bodies have not adapted to the state where we can handle the high amount of fiber contained in Alfalfa.

Although this amazing plant contains many of the vitamins and minerals known to mankind, the minerals are in trace amounts. Thus, Alfalfa cannot sustain human life.

The roots of this plant extend deep into the earth where it reaches mineral-rich soil—the secret to its high nutrient content. It is an excellent source of chlorophyll. Because of its high fiber level, this herb absorbs and carries out of the system poisons and other unwanted matter.

Alfalfa is a wholesome herb that can be used in the prevention of colon cancer.

Herbalists use Alfalfa to treat arthritis, gout, and bone and joint inflammation. When a person begins taking this herb, he must start with a low amount of tablets since it can have an almost explosive-like effect in the bowel. As the body gradually becomes accustomed to it over a period of time, it will enable the person to take more tables without the gastric upset.

HORSETAIL

Another good herb for the treatment of osteoporosis is Horsetail *(Equisetrum arvense)*. The botanical name is derived from two Latin words, *equus* meaning "horse" and *seta* meaning "bristle." The name is the result of the herb's peculiar bristled appearance at the stem joints. Since Horsetail is a strong astringent it may be used for both internal and external wounds. It has been used in Europe for hundreds of years as a diuretic aiding in kidney infection and dropsy. Externally, it has been used as an eye wash. Guatemalan Indians use this herb to treat various cancers. Some herbalists use Horsetail in decoctions, poultices, and infusions for the treatment of polyps, abdominal and even oral cancer.[4] It also has been used to treat diabetes.

Osteoporosis: The Case of the Shrinking Human

This herb is very good in the treatment of osteoporosis since it facilitates the body's use of calcium. It is very high in silica, which helps to strengthen fingernails and increase urine flow. Silica aids osteoporosis sufferers with body movement by allowing the bones to become more limber. Ever wonder why children are so physically energetic and limber? It's because children have high levels of silica, which allows them greater mobility and flexibility.

In Europe, studies have shown that fractured bones heal much faster when treated with this amazing herb.

NUTRIENTS THAT HELP IN THE FIGHT AGAINST OSTEOPOROSIS

It would be very wrong of me not to mention several nutrients that can aid in the treatment of both bone and joint disease, particularly osteoporosis.

An excellent example of how nutrients work together in order to function properly is found in calcium, phosphorus, and vitamins A, C, and D. Calcium needs vitamin A, C, D, and phosphorus while at the same time these others nutrients must have calcium to do their work. It is unwise to take calcium alone. It's important to know what vitamins to combine in order to obtain the maximum benefit.

It is estimated that 99 percent of your calcium is found in your bones and teeth. Only about 1 percent circulates in your body fluids and tissues. Calcium is needed to build strong bones, for blood

Miracle Herbal Cures

clotting, to activate enzymes (digestive juices) and to control the fluid that passes throughout cellular walls.

Calcium and phosphorous must exist in the proper proportion if they are to be used adequately. The ratio must be two-to-one, or twice as much calcium as a given amount of phosphorus. The presence of vitamin D aids to normalize this ratio and to sustain a proper balance. It becomes essential to get enough of vitamin D from such sources as cod liver oil, milk and—let's not forget—a good amount of sunshine.

Vertebra fractures that are a result of calcium deficiency cause height reduction. Height reduction is common among osteoporosis sufferers. Calcium is important to the nervous system as it helps in transporting electrical impulses of the nerves from one part of the body to another.

Without calcium, you would never be able to pull your hand away from a fire or move out of the way if someone was going to strike you. Heart palpitations can occur when the balance of calcium in the body is not sufficient. Leg cramps at night is another indication of low calcium.

Good sources of calcium are all dairy products and green vegetables such as broccoli, kale, collards, string beans and mustard greens. Another good source of calcium is bone meal. This is a supplement made from cattle bones and dried in a vacuum process so the minerals are not depleted. Bone meal is very good since other minerals are also present, while calcium-phosphorus is in perfect proportion. Another good source is calcium-fortified citrus juices. However, drink the juices in moderation since they tend to be high in sugar.

Osteoporosis: The Case of the Shrinking Human

The role of magnesium in preventing osteoporosis is very important. Magnesium is closely related to both calcium and phosphorus in its location and function in the body. About 70 percent of this mineral will be found in the bones, while the other 30 percent is in the soft tissues and the blood. It is interesting to note that the muscles of the human body contain more magnesium than calcium. Magnesium is necessary in starting various chemical reactions in the body.

This mineral plays an important role as a coenzyme in the building of protein. In addition to this, magnesium has a direct relationship with the hormone cortisone as they affect the amount of phosphate in the blood.[5]

Studies have proven that animals on a diet deficient in magnesium become extremely nervous. As a result, their responses become exaggerated even to small noises. However, such unnatural sensitiveness disappears when the mineral is supplied in sufficient amounts.

Proper amounts of phosphorus are needed in the prevention and treatment of osteoporosis. Phosphorus is found in all of the body cells. About 66 percent of body phosphorus is in the bones. It is known as calcium phosphate in the skeleton. About 33 percent of this mineral may be found in soft tissue as organic and inorganic phosphate.[6] Phosphorus converts oxidative energy to cells for better cellular functioning. Phosphorus will influence protein, carbohydrate and fat synthesis. In addition, it simulates muscular contraction, secretion of glandular hormones, nerve impulses and kidney functioning.

Phosphorus initiates internal energy. It functions to neutralize excess blood acidity. It helps create lecithin and cerebrin, ingredients needed for mental power. It aids the body in metabolizing both fats and starches.[7]

Too much white sugar interferes with the calcium-phosphorus balance in a person's body. A good source of phosphorus is found in bone meal. Your local health food store offers several products that give you the daily minimum balance.

So now that we have an overall pattern of what is needed for the prevention and treatment of osteoporosis, we must take intelligent steps to avoid this terrible disease.

Chapter Seven

New Hope for the Diabetic

Diabetes is a very common, but startling, disease that affects millions of Americans. Diabetes mellitus is a disorder in which the pancreas produces insufficient or virtually no insulin. Insulin is the hormone responsible for the absorption of glucose for energy needs and into the liver and fat cells for storage.[1] When this takes place the level of glucose in the blood becomes abnormally high, which causes excessive urination and a constant thirst and hunger. When the body is unable to utilize glucose, this causes weight loss and fatigue. Diabetes mellitus can cause a disordered lipid metabolism and accelerated degeneration of small blood vessels.[2]

Diabetes insipidus is more severe than diabetes mellitus and is usually present in younger people, especially teenagers.

There are two main types of diabetes mellitus. The first is "insulin dependent" Type 1 diabetes. Type 1 diabetes is the more severe form and first appears in people under the age of 35; it is most common between the ages of 10 and 16. Juvenile diabetes develops very rapidly whereas adult diabetes is gradual. The insulin-secreting cells in the pancreas are destroyed, resulting in a drastic decrease of insulin.

When the liver produces too much glucose and the pancreas produces too little insulin that is when we have the problem of diabetes. When the body is overloaded with high amounts of glucose, but the individual is not active enough to burn up the additional fuel, real problems develop.

Most often with diabetes the diet is the real problem. It is possible to alter diabetes in some cases if the diabetic is willing to change his diet and start exercising. Aside from diet and exercise, the diabetic must receive regular injections of insulin, otherwise he will lapse into a coma and die.

Excessive glucose can become most acidic and can lead to the destruction of certain nerve endings.[3] The eyes can be directly affected by eroding the nerve that enables the retinas to tear loose from their pods, the end result being blindness. Excessive glucose causes the blood to become sluggish, which slows the circulation process.

NATURE'S OWN MEDICINE

There are several herbs and minerals that can help prevent diabetes or help control the disease when it is present.

Juniper Berries *(juniperus supp.)* are excellent for nourishing and stimulating the pancreas to produce insulin.[4] It was believed during the Middle Ages that the scent of Juniper would ward off the plague. These berries have been used as a diuretic for centuries. In actual fact it is in the volatile oil where the active diuretic principles of the berries reside.[5]

Juniper berries are a moderate circulatory stimulant. Occasionally they have been used to treat rheumatic disorder when it was due to diminished circulation and general toxicity.

Juniper is very beneficial in helping to dissolve kidney stones and also prostate sediment. Through the centuries these berries have been helpful with patients suffering from water retention.

Kidney function is vastly increased by juniper. It creates urine flow and promotes the blood purification process.

Juniper berries will help prevent the crystallization of uric acid in the kidneys. Consequently, it remains in the solution as the acid is excreted.

Juniper aids in producing usable insulin in the healing effect on the entire body where there might be an insulin deficiency. We know that juniper is an excellent blood cleanser. At the same time it has the ability to tone the pancreas, providing the congestive conditions or other deleterious lymphatic damage has not progressed beyond the point of repair.[6]

If a diabetic takes juniper berries, there will be improvement over a period of weeks.

Golden Seal

Golden Seal *(Hydrastis canadensis)* was discovered and is found primarily in eastern North America and Canada. The Indians of Ohio found this herb to be most plentiful in the woods. The Cherokee Indians introduced Golden Seal as a medicine for the treatment of ulcers.[7] The effective chemical found in Golden Seal is hydrazine.

The amazing herb has a beneficial effect on the uterus by causing "uterine contractions." As a result, it has been useful in the treatment of bleeding from the uterus and for profuse menstruation.

Golden Seal when used with Licorice reduces high blood sugar levels and is most helpful in treating stress and anxiety.

This delightful herb is reported to strengthen the immune system since it contains antibiotic and antibacterial properties. The natural antibiotic, Berberine, which is found in Golden Seal, is excellent in treating mouth and gum problems.

This herb helps promote heart and respiratory function, increasing its capacity since it has the ability to clean mucous membranes and counter infection.[8]

Kelp

Kelp *(Fucus vesiclosus)* is a sea weed and is harvested off the coasts of many of the oceans of the world. States such as California and countries such as Norway harvest kelp on a regular basis. This amazing herb does so many wonderful things for the human body. Japanese studies now show a direct relationship between the ingestion of the algin (Kelp) contained in this herb, and the prevention of breast cancer and have concluded that algin is responsible.[9]

Kelp is full of iodine. Iodine is necessary for thyroid function, which controls metabolism. If the thyroid is underactive there will be weight gain. When properly supplemented, the thyroid functions normally and weight loss becomes possible.

Kelp is capable of reducing the risk of poisoning from environmental pollution by providing fiber that will increase fecal bulk. It has the buffering ability to neutralize wastes from the body fluids so that they may be discharged more readily from the body. This in turn will assist in reducing cholesterol levels.

Kelp contains all of the minerals, vitamins and cell salts in a concentrated form necessary for life. Kelp can stimulate the metabolism, which will strengthen all of the body systems. Perhaps all of us should be taking kelp tablets.

Studies have shown that kelp supplies hypotension and serum cholesterol lowering principles, which have an effect on cardia and neural tissues. This saves these tissues from unnecessary stress, increasing their efficiency.[10]

Acidity and a lack of essential nutrients for nerves and their insulating sheaths can lead to inflammation and neuritis. Kelp has those elements that help handle uric acid and eliminate it from the entire body system. Iodine contained in kelp acts as a tranquilizer and interrupts the disease chain.

In Asia, kelp is used to treat various genito-urinary tract problems. They also treat kidney, bladder, prostate and uterine problems with this outstanding herb. Men having prostate problems should take kelp on a daily basis to reduce the size of an enlarged prostate. Thus, urination becomes painless.

Chromium

Chromium is a trace mineral that assists in glucose metabolism. Many diabetics have low levels of this trace mineral or no level at all. Chromium helps maintain proper blood sugar levels and also aids in lowering LDL cholesterol levels and increasing HDL levels. It assists in preventing and lowering high blood pressure, improves cellular uptake of trace minerals and lessens age-related diseases. It increases strength and muscle mass and even may extend the human life span by slowing the primary aging processes.[11]

Chromium is necessary for diabetics as it improves glucose tolerance. Studies show that chromium delays the appearance of age-related heart disease and adult-onset diabetes, and even strokes. This trace mineral can help prevent hypoglycemia and hyperglycemia.

Chromium is part of the Glucose Tolerance Factor (GTF), helping to break up and even dissolve excessive cholesterol and triglycerides.[12]

Since the soil in our northern States is virtually deplete of this necessary trace mineral, it would be advisable for northerners to take chromium supplementation.

OTHER ESSENTIAL HERBS

L-glutamine is an essential amino acid that helps reduce the craving for sweets and may even help alleviate some anxiety.

We have also mentioned in previous chapters the herb called Dandelion Root. This incredible herb benefits the liver because it helps cleanse the liver from toxic poisons. Inasmuch as the conversion of nutrients takes place in the liver, we must keep the liver clean so that it might function as best as possible.

Another important mineral needed for sugar facilitation is zinc. We have previously mentioned zinc but must stress how important it is for the formation of insulin. Without normal levels of zinc, diabetes is almost going to manifest itself.

Vitamin B_3, or niacinamide, is wonderful for opening up the vascular system. It allows an increased flow of blood to the eyes, arms, legs and toes. Niacinamide is a synthetic form of niacin. This wonderful vitamin helps with blood circulation and reducing the levels of serum cholesterol. Lean meats, poultry, fish and peanuts are very good sources of this vitamin.

Vitamin F, which is found in pumpkin seeds, aids in dissolving fatty acid deposits. It also helps the body convert glucose into energy. Its function is very similar to that of vitamin B_1.

There is so much that you can do for yourself if you suffer from diabetes. However, even when trying alternative medicine, never stop taking your insulin unless directed by your physician to do so.

Chapter Eight

God's Natural Prozac

Depression is a commonly occurring problem. It is estimated that about 17 percent of all Americans suffer from some form of depression. The very nature of depression involves a mixture of severity, length and mode of treatment. This becomes rather difficult for doctors to treat. Since there are numerous side effects from anti-depressant drugs, it would seem logical that there should be non-drug alternatives.

Literally millions of people at one time or another will suffer from mild to moderate depression. Before taking a doctor's prescription for an anti-depressant, why not consider taking St. John's Wort? Ask your medical practitioner for his opinion of this herb. St. John's Wort is used extensively in

Europe and outsells all other anti-depressants—even Prozac—by more than seven-to-one.[1]

There have been twenty-five tests done in Germany on this herb. The findings indicated that St. John's Wort relieves depression often as effectively as strong anti-depressant drugs and does not present the unpleasant side effects as other drugs do.

Finally, American doctors and government officials are becoming excited about St. John's Wort as a benign, but potent, treatment for mild to moderate depression.

The European findings are so exciting that the National Institute of Mental Health is starting to break ground on a new clinical study to prove the effectiveness of St. John's Wort. If this herb really works as the Europeans believe, then millions of Americans will be able to take it without the fear of side effects. It is now available in most pharmacies across the United States. Consult a good naturopathic physician before starting on this herbal program.

There is very little risk in using St. John's Wort for a range of symptoms and problems. In Germany, St. John's Wort is licensed for the treatment of "anxiety and depressive and sleep disorders." In 1993, there were over 2.7 million prescriptions issued in Germany for St. John's Wort for the treatment of depression.

Aside from depression, St. John's Wort (Hypericum) acts as a powerful antiviral agent. This herb recently has gained much attention from the medical world because of its effectiveness against a range of viruses and retroviruses. The effective virucidal activity evolves from a combination of photodynamic and lipophilic properties.[2] An article in the journal *Transfusion,* explains how hypericin (the depression fighting compound found in St. John's Wort) actually works in inhibiting viral activity in cells:

> Hypericin binds cell membranes (and, by inference, virus membranes) and crosslinks virus capsid proteins. This action results in a loss of infectivity and an inability to retrieve the reverse transcriptase enzymatic activity from the virion.[3]

In 1991, there were various studies carried out that focused on hypericin's ability to inhibit viral activity. These dealt specifically with the murine cytomegalovirus (MCMV) and Sindbis virus. The inactivated MCMV, when used in infected cells, was totally unable to synthesize early or late viral antigens. When hypericin was added to cells infected with viable MCMV, there was a direct inhibition observed, especially when the compound was administered in the first two hours of infection.[4]

Studies have shown that hypericin appears to have two modes of antiviral activity: "...one directed at the virions, possibly on membranes components, and the other directed at virus-infected cells. Both activities are substantially enhanced by light."[5]

There have been studies done on St. John's Wort and how it relates to training AIDS/HIV. In 1991, *Science* magazine reported on the first study using the isolated hypericin, a key compound in Hypericum (St. John's Wort).[6] Fred Valentine and Howard Hochster, researchers at New York University Medical Center, studied the effects at how hypericin can help uninfected T-cells from being infected with the AIDS virus in a cell culture. The study showed that hypericin can precisely target new virus particles and prevent them from infecting other cells.[7]

There are two drugs that have been approved by the FDA for the treatment of HIV infection—AZT and DDL. These work by interfering with the key viral enzyme: reverse transcriptase. Tests show that hypericin can be effective at reversing the transcriptase phase, and can work synergistically with other AIDS drugs. This herb truly has a most remarkable propensity to various things that other herbs can not even begin to match.

Another study valued the use and attitudes of HIV sufferers concerning the use of more alternative treatments for the virus as opposed to clinical drug therapies. The medical world has no cure at this time for AIDS, yet St. John's Wort was considered as being most valued. So many people are turning to the world of herbs and finding that they are getting good results.

Various other studies done around America have been published in *Photochemistry-Photobiology* and have given hypericin an upperhand over the hypocrellins in treating HIV. This is just one more feather in the cap for St. John's Wort.[8]

St. John's Wort has shown itself to be effective in treating sleep disorders. As we get older many find sleeping to become rather difficult. Insomnia, intermittent waking, sleep duration and overall poor sleeping qualities respond quite well to St. John's Wort. The traditional medical world has countless pills to assist in sleeping disorders, but these drugs have side effects. In 1994, a double-blind study was conducted and the results were published in the *Journal of Geriatric Psychiatry and Neurology*. The study showed that St. John's Wort extracts increased sleep during the total period of sleep for the patient. Again, this is more good news for this amazing wonder herb.

In addition, to St. John's Wort has been used to aid in wound healing. As early as the Crusades, this herb was used in the treatment of sword and various other wounds. It was used as an oil, which does not contain hypericin, but contains another valuable compound called hyperforin.[9] This chemical is most useful as a primary component in salves or dressings for topical and other wounds. It has the properties to withstand and inhibit bacterial and viral growths.

St. John's Wort also can work against cancerous cells and tumors of various kinds.

The publication *Laryngyscope* reports that St. John's Wort is having great effectiveness in targeting human cancer growth. This is done through a process that is laser activated by using St. John's Wort in conjunction with other cancer drugs.[10] This causes improved inhibition of cancerous growths and their cells. The study has stated the following:

> These results show that hypericin is a sensitive agent for phototherapy of human cancer cells in vitro and indicate that this

drug may be useful for tumor targeting via minimally invasive imaging-guided laser fiber optics.[11]

This outstanding herb has so many good benefits that it might actually, in the future, present itself as a form of cancer cure for various tumor-type cancers. Further research will definitely tell us about its properties and abilities in cancer treatment.

There needs to be a word of caution when using St. John's Wort since it has been shown to demonstrate a side effect producing photosensitivity. Clinical studies show that hypericin is absorbed in the intestines and concentrates near the skin. An allergic reaction can take place when those with fair skin are exposed directly to sunlight. This type of exposure can cause tissue damage and even death in some cases. Those taking this herb must take care to keep out of the sun.

St. John's Wort has been used with great success for chronic fatigue syndrome and even mental burnout. There are those in the medical profession who believe there is no such thing as chronic fatigue syndrome, but that is purely their opinion and not mine.

This herb is known to relieve phlegm obstruction in the chest and lungs. It is excellent in the treatment of bronchitis and is known to vanish all signs of disease.

There are studies in Europe that have demonstrated the ability of St. John's Wort to suppress internal bleeding. It is very beneficial in chronic uterine problems and will aid in correcting irregular and painful menstruation.

Miraculous Herbal Cures

and put meaning back into his life. St. John's Wort—I call it "God's natural Prozac."

Again, St. John's Wort is a powerful herb that must be used with discretion. Before taking this herb, it is best to consult a respected naturopathic physician. Most medical doctors know nothing about it. A naturopathic physician can tell you how much you need or don't need. Consult with them before starting any herbal program.

Chapter Nine

God's Miracle Cure for the Prostate

If you are a man over the age of fifty and living in the United States, it is most likely that you have an enlarged prostate gland, medically known as benign prostatic hyperplasis (BPH). It is certain that as these men get older, their condition can escalate. Although this condition is harmless, it does cause great discomfort. A swollen prostate can squeeze the urethra, interfering with normal urination. Symptoms include frequent nighttime trips to the bathroom, serious pain from the obstruction of urinary flow and trouble with erections.

If there is a change in urinary habits, please see a physician as soon as possible. If the urine is not flowing freely, it can cause urinary infection or even the risk of kidney infection or cystitis. Surgery may be necessary if the urine outflow is blocked.

The prostate is a small gland located around the urethra at the point where it leaves the bladder. We aren't totally aware of what the prostate actually does. We do know that it secretes a fluid that assists the movement of sperm after ejaculation.

Most importantly, an enlarged prostate can indicate possible cancer of this gland. This is why it's so important for men, especially over age fifty, to have regular check-ups. Early detection of any cancer can save a life.

THERE ARE SEVERAL HERBS THAT DO HELP WITH PROSTATE HEALTH

Saw Palmetto *(Serenoa repens)* is an old American tonic that dates back to the Maya Indians and perhaps even further. The Saw Palmetto berry has been used for centuries to treat various diseases of the genito-urinary system. European scientists have conducted studies indicating the effects of this wonderful berry in relationship to BPH (benign prostatic hyperplasia). European physicians believe that testosterone levels build up in the prostate. When this happens, the testosterone in the prostate is converted to a very potent compound called "dihydrotestosterone." This compound causes cells to multiply very rapidly, which results in an enlarged prostate. Studies have proven that Saw Palmetto berries prevent the conversion of testosterone into dihydrotestosterone. Saw Palmetto berries are fat-soluble.

When Saw Palmetto is found in herbal combinations, the berries can be an appetite stimulate, improves digestion, assimilation and provide the necessary nutrition for the diabetic condition. It also is helpful for other glands of the body.

Saw Palmetto aids in reducing the inflammation and pain associated with an enlarged prostate gland. It increases the bladder's ability to contract and even expel its contents.[1] Saw Palmetto is found in every formula for male impotence, sterility and reproductive problems.[2] It is definitely known to increase blood flow to the sexual organs.

This incredible herb actually assists the thyroid to regulate sexual development. At the same time the herb will normalize the activity of those glands and organs. Many herbalists recommend Saw Palmetto in nearly all cases of wasting diseases since it has an effect upon glandular tissues.[3]

This herb is very quieting to the nerves and acts as an antiseptic. Saw palmetto also can relieve excessive mucus in the head and nose and helps in the cases of chronic bronchitis and asthma.

Once we had a guest speaker come to our church who was suffering from an enlarged prostate gland. His doctor had told him it could be cancerous and that he would have to undergo surgery and radiation. Naturally, this gentleman was greatly anxious about this condition, realizing he would have quite a battle on his hands.

I told him that I did not believe his enlarged prostate was cancerous nor did I think he would need to have surgery. I put him on a product produced by the Vitamine Shoppe called "Prosta Guard" and zinc. The prostate gland needs zinc supplementation on a daily basis since it is mostly made of zinc. After just a few short weeks, the report came back from his doctor.

Miracle Herbal Cures

This gentleman told me, "You will be glad to know that when I saw the consulting doctor at the hospital, he found that my prostate had shrunk considerably and has told me to come back in six months. There was no need to worry. My PSI had dropped from 8 to 4.9, and I believe that it is still dropping."

When herbs are used properly the results can be miraculous. We need to know what we must have for our bodies and the proper amount of this herb. This then will give our bodies the means to heal naturally.

Saw Palmetto is very good for impotence. Just look at the popular success of Viagra, the sometimes dangerous prescription drug, and you realize how widespread this problem is. Basically it is the inability to maintain an erection for a long enough period of time during intercourse.

There are numerous causes of impotence, some of which are psychological and others might be hormonal. What we do know is that the penis must have a good blood supply for an erection. We also know that the arteries supplying that part of the body are subject to narrowing and blocking just like any other part of the body. When there is a blockage, this impairs circulation and affects the possibility of an erection. There are several other herbs that also have positive effects on this intimate function.

Damiana leaves are very helpful for impotent problems and are safe enough to take up to three times a day. They are available in most good health food stores, and it is best to take them in capsule form.

Again, Ginkgo Biloba is a good herb that helps supply blood to the area of the penis. A scientific study in the *Journal of Urology* showed that ginkgo improved the blood flow to the penis in men who had narrowing of the arteries that supply blood to this organ.[4]

In this study, men took 60 milligrams of ginkgo per day. By the end of the year, half of them were totally healed. Any man who experiences an occasional bout of impotence should take ginkgo. If the problem persists, it is best to see a specialist who treats this kind of disorder. Today, as never before, help and effective treatments are available.

Chapter Ten

God's Natural Aspirin

A woman suffered from migraines for more than twenty years. They would usually strike about once a week making life almost impossible. She would spend her weekends in bed, hoping to be ready for work by Monday morning. Her husband and children all knew that Mother was not able to be with them at that time. This became a great tragedy for this lady since she deeply loved her two little girls and desperately wanted to be part of their lives in a greater way. The migraines were so awful that everybody in the house feared them. She suffered all the classic symptoms—visual disturbances, light sensitivity, slurred speech, throbbing head pain and ungodly nausea. There were days when all she could do was just sit in the bathroom.

Miracle Herbal Cures

Naturally, she tried every conceivable means of orthodox medicine. There were times when her husband would take her to the emergency room of the local hospital for a shot to stop the horrific pain. She tried Inderal, a beta blocker used to treat high blood pressure and rapid heart beat, and often prescribed for the treatment of migraines. But this didn't work in her case. She visited a chiropractor and tried that for a long period of time with very little success. She periodically visited her medical doctor when she knew that a headache was approaching. He would give her an injection of sumatriptan (Imitrex) to ward off the agonizing pain. The shot helped immensely, but would soon wear off. One day in the health food store she was introduced to the herb Feverfew quite by accident. She bought a bottle of it and her headaches gradually disappeared—and so did the conventional medicine. Eventually, her migraines disappeared for good.

She spends about ten cents per day on the herb. It comes in a easy-to-swallow capsule and has no side effects. As an attorney's secretary, her boss was amazed at the results he witnessed in his office. She became a "delight to work with," according to her boss and co-workers. Those dark days have truly passed and now she is able to live the life she always wanted.

There are various causes for migraine headaches, such as consuming too much white sugar products, coffee, alcohol or tobacco. Other causes of migraines include mental tension such as grief, rage and anxiety. Glandular deficiencies, wrong eating habits, constipation and certain odors or inhalants can trigger the headache. Even food preservatives found in cheese, milk, chocolate, pork and wine can cause a migraine.

If you have ever suffered from a migraine you know that an aspirin is just about useless against these ferocious headaches. But God has provided a secret potion that can stop such debilitating headaches. Those that have used "Feverfew" over a period of time will tell you that this herb is a "miracle pill." It costs about ten cents per pill with the awesome power to turn off those ugly, painful headaches that affect about 23 million Americans.

Feverfew *(Chrysanthemum parthenium)* has been known since the Middle Ages and has been used as a herb to reduce fevers. Feverfew is a common feathery plant, and is a member of the daisy family. The word *Feverfew* comes from the Latin *febrifugia*, which literally means "driver out of fevers."[1] Ancient Greeks used this herb for the beneficial effects it had on the uterus. If contractions were not regular in childbirth, the herb would be administered to bring about regular contractions. It also was used in the first century as a pain reliever for arthritic conditions.

Tens of thousands of migraine sufferers will tell you about the benefits of using this herb for alleviating the nausea and vomiting that often accompany these headaches. It is interesting to note that the word *migraine* comes from the Greek language and means "half of the skull," since the excruciating pain usually strikes one side of the cranium.[2] Research has shown that Feverfew is far more effective than aspirin in relieving the pain of a migraine.

Miracle Herbal Cures

Many herbalists are of the opinion that Feverfew should be taken on a daily basis to prevent migraine. They believe that taking the herb during the headache itself is to limit the benefits of this herb. In other words, the herb should be taken consistently on a daily basis for prevention and best results.

Researchers have determined that the extracts of Feverfew inhibit the production of prostaglandins, which constrict and dilate cerebral blood vessels, causing migraine headaches.

Feverfew aids the body in healing itself and is a great natural way to strengthen the body. In addition to all of its benefits, Feverfew restores normal liver function.

In the early 1600s, British doctors heralded Feverfew as "very effectual for all pains (sic) in the head."[3] In 1772, John Hill, a British physician, stated in his book *The Family Herbal:* "In the worst headache this herb exceeds whatever else is known." For some unknown reason, Feverfew fell into disuse for a few centuries. It is not as effective against fever as it was once thought. It became popular in the 1980s in England when researchers discovered it had a potent chemical beneficial for treating migraines.

While living in England, we heard about Mrs. Jenkins, whose husband is the president of Britain's National Coal Board. At the age of sixty-eight she began chewing three leaves of Feverfew on a daily basis. Within a ten-month period, her migraines had completely disappeared.

Mrs. Jenkins's medical doctor, Dr. Johnson, was so impressed with her results that he contacted the

London Migraine Clinic and discovered that over 300 patients who had been using Feverfew for migraines reported similar results.[4] Consequently, studies were done that proved Feverfew actually cures migraines.

In 1985, Dr. Johnson wrote in the *British Medical Journal* his conclusions, which had involved studying 270 suffers of migraine. Those who habitually took Feverfew were migraine-free. Those who took it occasionally had headaches, but they were fewer in number and more mild in nature. Those who were given a placebo suffered from migraines, but those given the capsule with Feverfew were migraine-free.

More clinical evidence came as the results of a so-called double-blind controlled study of migraine sufferers who had never taken Feverfew previously. In 1988, researchers from the University Hospital of Nottingham, England, recorded in the British medical journal, *The Lancet,* that those taking Feverfew over a period of four months became migraine-free. Those who were given dried cabbage leaves in capsule form were suffering as usual from migraines. The tests showed beyond any shadow of a doubt that Feverfew is an excellent herb for the treatment of migraine headaches.

The chemical found in Feverfew is parthenolide—an anti-migraine agent. Feverfew has high concentrations of this chemical that gives it such healing properties. When there is an excess of serotonin, a hormone active in cells and blood vessels of the brain, this can trigger a migraine. Most likely serotonin causes a constriction of blood vessels in the brain.

Miracle Herbal Cures

Feverfew has an anti-inflammatory effect that may prevent migraines. Studies at Nottingham University also showed that Feverfew's complex mixture of chemicals are "high potency" inhibitors of thromboxane B_2 and leukotriene B_4, which foster inflammation and pain. Feverfew can actually block these inflammatory chemicals by 58 percent, according to test tube studies.[5] The herb also has an antithrombotic activity, antibacterial activity and anti-allergic activity. It actually inhibits mast cell release of histamine.

While Feverfew capsules are sold just about everywhere today, do not exceed the recommended dosage on the bottle. Most bottles will tell you to take three capsules daily. This is fine in the beginning, but it is best to cut down to one capsule a day. This will help prevent the onset of migraines. There are very few side effects from taking this herb. In about 8 percent of all users, some may suffer from minor mouth sores and gastrointestinal upset. The herb is considered non-toxic but there have been no long-term studies done. Some naturopathic doctors advise against using Feverfew with over-the-counter drugs such as Motrin, Advil, aspirin and even Tylenol. It is believed these can reduce the herb's effectiveness.

Since Feverfew causes uterine contractions, lactating mothers and children under two years of age should not take this herb. Also, if you are taking an anti-coagulants drug, you should not take this herb. Feverfew has the propensity of thinning the blood.

The British use Feverfew to help relieve the pain of rheumatoid arthritis. When rheumatoid arthritis

God's Natural Aspirin

flares up, the cells are filled with leukotrienes. There are constituents in Feverfew that help alleviate the symptoms.[6] Unfortunately, the British have not done any long-term studies on Feverfew and its relationship to rheumatoid arthritis.

The leaves of Feverfew are very bitter and are hard to chew. It is best to buy the standardized capsules or pills sold at the health food shop. Here in Minnesota, Feverfew tables are sold at our local grocery stores.

Feverfew should be your herb of choice if you suffer from migraine headaches.

Chapter Eleven

God's Best Herbs for Anxiety

Anxiety is the modern American ailment and the result of too much stress. It is so common that we have accepted it as a normal part of our daily life. The truth of the matter is that there's nothing funny about anxiety especially when you are in its grips. It should be understood that anxiety is not natural, and we don't have to live with it.

Most psychologists will tell you that the antidote to anxiety is a time of relaxation and inner tranquillity. There are various methods to accomplish this. One of the best ways I know is to enter into the presence of God and meditate on His Word.

> Do not be anxious about anything, but in everything, by prayer and petition,

> with thanksgiving, present your requests to God. And the peace of God, which transcends all understanding will guard your hearts and minds in Christ Jesus.
>
> —Philippians 4:6-7, NIV

At other times, additional means are necessary to help you overcome this sense of disquietness. There might be a need to start supplementing your diet with various herbs to help reduce the feelings of anxiety.

I am sure that most of us know all about tranquilizers. For numerous years in America they've been the drug of choice by most medical doctors. Valium, Xanax and Placodil are among the mainstays of American drug therapy. These drugs will definitely relax you, but they have certain harmful side effects. These drugs are addictive, they can impair your mental abilities, slow your reflexes, damage the liver and leave you in generally poor health.

Herbs provide a safer alternative for those experiencing stress and anxiety.

The following herbs can soothe frayed nerves and even calm you down. Unlike their synthetic counterparts, they will not have severe narcotic side effects.

Everybody now and then has a sleepless night. Insomnia is far more prevalent than most people realize. At times you might have trouble falling asleep or perhaps wake up in the middle of the night and have difficulty returning to sleep. If this persists for more than a night or two, it could be an indication that you are suffering from unresolved stress, tension or perhaps even worry.

There are times when we need to examine ourselves. All of us need our own personal business meeting with our conscience. Take time to examine your circumstances, and if there is a troublesome problem, get to the bottom of it. Stop drinking too much coffee, tea and caffeinated drinks. If the insomnia continues, then it is best to seek medical attention as it could be a symptom of a deeper and even serious condition.

The following will help for the occasional bout of insomnia.

The herb "Passion Flower" contains several chemicals of a varied nature that exert a calming and tranquilizing effect both on the brain and the body.

Passion Flower *(passiflora incarnata)* gets its name from the finely cut corona found in the very center of its blossom. It resembles the crown of thorns given to Jesus Christ during His scourging in the pretorian guard room. Passion Flower is a symbol of Christ's crucifixion. During the seventeenth century it was professed to be seen by the early Jesuit priests and other explorers from Spain and Italy. They interpreted this as a sign of divine guidance for the success of their efforts to convert the natives to Roman Catholicism.[1]

Passion Flower was greatly used by North American Indian tribes for the healing of earaches, boils and other inflammations. The Mayan Indians of Yucatan, Mexico, used this herb to treat insomnia, hysteria and convulsions.

Especially in Italy, Passion Flower has been used to treat hyperactive children. The results have been truly amazing in calming down these children. The herb has shown itself to be effective in treating nervous problems with children such as muscle twitching and irritability and is beneficial in aiding their concentration at school.

This amazing herb has been used primarily as a motor nerve depressant as it lowers motor nerve activity. It aids in respiration and produces a temporary reduction of blood pressure. It does improve circulation and helps with the nutrition of the nerve centers.

Passion Flower also is beneficial for women experiencing PMS (premenstrual syndrome). It helps in quieting the woman as her hormones are temporarily out of balance.

This herb is very rich in flavonoids. It is effective in combinations to overcome alcohol abuse without the morning hangover. Passion Flower does possess an analgesic (painkiller) and anti-inflammatory properties, to assist in sleeplessness caused by brain inflammations. This herb is helpful in aiding those who desire to come off of synthetic sleeping pills and tranquilizers.

It is known that Passion Flower kills the bacteria that causes eye irritations and has surpassed the effectiveness of commercial products.

DO NOT DRIVE OR OPERATE ANY MACHINERY AFTER TAKING PASSION FLOWER. This is a very important warning because Passion Flower acts like a tranquilizer.

Another excellent herb for calming the central nervous system is Skullcap. Skullcap *(Scutellaria lateriflora)* is the popular and generic name derived from the Latin *scutella*, which means "a small dish" in reference to the shape of the extremities of the flower. It was known as Mad Dogweed since it was considered in olden times to be are remedy for hydrophobia (rabies).[2]

This herb calms the nervous system without narcotic properties. It quiets the person and assists in bringing about natural sleep.

Most herbalists will inform you that skullcap is an excellent nervine. It acts upon the central and sympathetic nervous system to help control most nervous irritations. It gives a sense of well being and inner calm, which in turn allows relaxed sleep.

This herb is most helpful for those who have given up addictions such as drugs and alcohol. It has wonderful detoxification properties that tends to lessen the severity of withdrawal symptoms, such as delirium tremors.[3]

Skullcap has been used for hundreds of years for its abilities in spasmodic affliction such as St. Vitus Dance (involuntary jerking motion). It also aids in quieting the nerves after an epileptic seizure.

It is excellent in treating neurasthenia, a disease following depression in which the person suffers from chronic exhaustion.

You can make skullcap tea with one tablespoon of the herb in two cups of boiling water. Let it steep for ten minutes, strain and drink it before bedtime. There are skullcap capsules that can be taken before bedtime.

WARNING: DO NOT DRIVE OR OPERATE MACHINERY AFTER TAKING SKULLCAP.

Valerian is another outstanding herb for the treatment of nervous disorders. The name usually reminds us of a very popular tranquilizer called

Miracle Herbal Cures

Valium. Valerian *(Valeriana officinalis)* has been used for many centuries to calm all kinds of nervous disorders. This herb slows the action of the heart, but increases the power of the stroke of the heart.

Valerian root is primarily a sedative and is used when there are sleeping disorders related to anxiety, nervousness, exhaustion, headache or hysteria. Valerian root has been used long before the time of Christ and is cited in virtually every herbal pharmacopoeia worldwide.

Valerian root influences the cerebrospinal system and is used as a sedative of the primary nerve centers for afflictions such as St. Vitus Dance, nervous jerking motions, neuralgia pain, epileptic seizures, hysteria, restlessness and wakefulness.

The herb plays an important role in the process of rehabilitation for many addicts. Occasionally it will serve as a substitute for valium in aiding better sleep for the addict. It mellows out the individual and allows for overall relaxation. It has been used effectively for cases of hysteria and hypochondria where the initial causes were emotional.

Herbalists often use valerian to help cause a substantial reduction in heart palpitation. It has been used for circulatory problems and effects the stomach and intestinal motility.

It is a marvelous herb since it helps in so many numerous ways. It has been around for hundreds of years and used safely through the centuries.

DO NOT OPERATE MACHINERY OR DRIVE AFTER TAKING THIS HERB!

It is imperative to understand that the above herbs are not addictive and have very few side effects. Nevertheless, they are very potent and should be used only as directed; never exceed the recommended dosage.

Chapter Twelve

Helpful Herbs for Allergies

According to the Centers for Disease Control and Prevention, it is estimated that over 40 million Americans suffer from one type of allergy or another. Allergies come about as the immune system perceives a normally harmless substance, such as dust or pollen, as an invading irritant. As a result, this prompts the immune system to initiate a defensive chemical reaction that leads to the release of powerful substances known as histamines, which bombard the invading chemicals.

Depending upon where in the body the histamines are released, they will cause swelling and inflammation as well as a number of other allergic symptoms. Histamines cause the nasal passages to become congested; in the air passages the end

Miracle Herbal Cures

result is asthma; in the skin, hives and even eczema; in the joint linings, arthritis; and in the brain, headaches.

There are countless over-the-counter prescription drugs that aid in relieving allergic reactions, but at a very high price to overall health. The following herbs can make a great difference in the battle against allergies.

Eyebright *(Euphrasia officinalis)* has been known for hundreds of years for its healing power for the eyes. At the same time it is beneficial to relieve sore, itchy eyes due to allergies. It is excellent for those who suffer from hay fever.

Herbalists believe that the ancients knew of Eyebright's healing powers since the name *Euphrasia* is of Greek origin, stemming from *Euphrosyne,* meaning "gladness." It is thought that the plant acquired this name because of its well-known reputation for curing eye ailments.[1]

Through the centuries, Eyebright has been used as the herb of choice for numerous afflictions of the eye. This herb is especially good for aiding in healing problems relating to mucous membranes. It is helpful in both acute and chronic eye inflammations and has antiseptic properties for fighting eye infections. It is beneficial for those who suffer from light sensitivity, weak eyesight and weeping conditions as well.

When the herb is used as an oil to place upon the eye, it becomes activated by sunlight to work on the cornea, ciliary muscle, iris, ligaments, lens, retina and optic nerves. It then strengthens and soothes these areas, often improving eyesight and also has been used both to inhibit and reverse cataracts.

Helpful Herbs for Allergies

This amazing herb will work as a vaso-constrictor and astringent to the nasal and conjunctiva mucous.[2] It works wonderfully for tired and sore eyes. At the same time, it helps with eyes that are cloudy and irritated by lacrymation (excessive tears) of watery and stringy mucus.

At the same time it is helpful to take vitamin C along with the Eyebright. Vitamin C works to detoxify the blood by picking up proteins that do not belong in the system. When taken with vitamin E, vitamin C acts as an antihistamine.

Nettle *(Urtica dioica)* is an old folk remedy that works for hay fever and other allergies. This Stinging nettle was cultivated in Scotland for the fibers in the stalks to make very durable linen-like cloth. This ancient practice actually goes back to the Bronze Age. The name *Nettle* is derived from words meaning "textile plant."[3]

Stinging nettle was used as an agent that, by irritating the area of skin that was inflamed, would increase blood flow to that very area.

Aside from its treatment for allergies, nettle has numerous other healing properties. Nettle is marvelous for the treatment of gout. It neutralizes uric acid, prevents its crystallization aiding in its elimination from the system. This in turn does relieve gout and arthritis.

Nettle stops diarrhea and dysentery. It is especially good in treating inflammatory skin conditions.

The ancients used nettle as a remedy for dandruff and help in bringing back the natural color of hair. Nettle has been used to stop menses flow.

Nettle has been known to help correct thyroid conditions such as low thyroid. This amazing herb helps in cleansing the digestive tract and with stomach problems.

This herb is especially rich in minerals and is most beneficial during pregnancy. It has a high level of vitamin K that guards against excessive bleeding. It is excellent in improving kidney function and helps in the prevention of hemorrhoids.[4]

However, do not take nettle if you have high blood pressure.

Reishi Mushroom is delicious and very popular in Oriental cuisine for its powerful medicinal properties. In China and Korea, studies indicate that it has a strong antihistamine action that can help control allergies.

The latest research indicates that Reishi Mushroom is showing success against chronic fatigue syndrome by very noticeable increases of energy after its administration. This mushroom has been found to regenerate the liver, aids in lowering cholesterol and triglycerides, reduces coronary symptoms and high blood pressure. It can relieve some allergic reactions.

This herb has been found to protect against several kinds of cancer, increases vitality and strengthens the internal organs. It even improves conditions due to viral hepatitis. It has been known to improve insomnia by enhancing muscle relaxation. It aids in heart disease by lowering cholesterol and improves the coronary arteries.

This mushroom is a powerful immune-stimulating agent. It is very effective against degenerative diseases, such as cancer and AIDS. And it is helpful in reducing the side effects of cancer treatment.

Reishi bolsters the immune system, stimulates health and certainly improves (or even prevents) allergenic conditions.

It should be noted that Reishi may cause dizziness, sore bones, itchy skin, increase bowel movements and harden feces.[5] Pimple-like eruptions may occur during the initial intake period of starting with the mushroom, but these symptoms will disappear after a short period of time.

It is interesting to note that Reishi is an antioxidant. It can be used therapeutically for more serious conditions, including anti-tumor and anti-hepatitis activity.[6]

Please note that this mushroom can assist in numerous ways in healing, but it should be used with caution. Use it in moderation since it could possibly elevate your copper levels that could be detrimental.

It is necessary to be cautious when using any of these herbal preparations. Remember, herbs are powerful medicines that can be detrimental if taken in large doses or if abused.

Chapter Thirteen

The Miracle of Licorice

It would be a profound blessing for mankind if someone could find a definite cure for chronic fatigue syndrome. It would bring an end to the misery of literally millions of people around the world. chronic fatigue syndrome, also known as CFS, may actually be something you are not totally aware of. This disease is not a normal state of tiredness. All of us get tired at different times, but that isn't CFS. This disease has a cluster of flu-like symptoms, accompanied by headaches, joint and muscle pain, depression. Most of all, CFS's continuous fatigue can keep a person away from their work and in bed most of the day—all from no logical apparent cause. Normal medical treatment includes painkillers and antidepressants or any

Miracle Herbal Cures

other medicine the physician might deem meritable. Recovery from this disease is very rare and the frustration from it is enormous.

An article in *Consumer Reports* magazine observed: "Probably hundreds of thousands of people in the U.S. have chronic fatigue syndrome. Theories about the cause cover just about everything, including hormonal, immunological and neurological abnormalities. The ailment is every bit as baffling as it is devastating."

There is in nature an intriguing possibility that one of the oldest known herbs to mankind might be the cure to CFS. As new research is emerging, we are now able to understand the different mechanisms that trigger this disorder. Licorice often times helps relieve the numerous symptoms associated with CFS. Low blood pressure is a contributing factor to this disease, and licorice is an effective yet benign drug in treating this symptom. It certainly can be a miracle cure for many sufferers of CFS.

Licorice *(Glycyrrhiza glabra)* has been around for many centuries and was used by the troops of Alexander the Great. They would chew this herb in the midst of battle because it quenched their thirst and gave them bursts of energy. The chief active principle in licorice is glycrrhizic acid, which is fifty times sweeter than sugar cane, but does not increase thirst.

Glycyrrhiza is derived from the Greek words *glukus* meaning "sweet" and *riza* meaning "root" and refers to the fact that the dried roots can be chewed like a piece of candy.

Yet, the kind of licorice I'm talking about is vastly different from the kind of licorice children

The Miracle of Licorice

like to chew on. The licorice with healing properties is deglycrrhizinated licorice, or DGL.

Licorice root possesses substantial anti-arthritic properties that can relieve the pain and discomfort of this disease. It actually causes the release of corticoids from the adrenals and their anti-inflammatory properties then help reduce the discomfort of arthritis.

Licorice root effects the concentration of blood salts and stimulates and sustains adrenal function. At the same time, this root protects the liver from liver disease and cirrhosis.

Licorice has a definite propensity for regulating blood sugar levels. At the same time, if taken in large doses, it can cause sodium retention, potassium depletion and can lead to hypertension and even edema. Certain individuals who must be careful about using this herb since it will elevate their blood pressure. It is best to measure your blood pressure on a daily basis if you are using licorice.

Licorice is also excellent in healing inflamed mucous membranes of the respiratory tract and has been found in cough syrups and cough drops for hundreds of years. It is effective in treating symptoms of the common cold.

Licorice also has the ability to literally zap canker sores. Dr. Michael Traub, a naturopathic doctor, says, "DGL [deglycrrhizinated licorice] has anti-inflammatory properties. It speeds the healing process and soothes the discomfort of canker sores." Traub is the director of the integrated residency program at North Hawaii Community Hospital in Kamuela, Hawaii.

Miracle Herbal Cures

In one of Traub's studies, twenty people with recurrent canker sores used DGL mouthwash. It was noted that fifteen people experienced at least a 50 percent improvement within only one day. By the third day all of the patients were free of canker sores.

One of the young men in the study had recurrent canker sores for over ten years. He had various sores on his tongue, lips, inside his cheek, on his soft palate, and in the back of the throat. On the seventh day of treatment with DGL, the patient was totally free of canker sores.[1]

To initiate the healing process, take two 200-milligram tablets about twenty minutes before each meal, says Traub, or chew one or both tablets three times a day. You are than able to concentrate the tablets over the sores, which will even further speed up the healing.

It also is possible to empty the powder from a capsule into half a cup of lukewarm water, dissolve the DGL, and swish the solution around in your mouth. Repeat this process at least three times a day until the sores are gone.

Licorice acts as a turbo charge to the immune system and builds resistance against the herpes virus. Glycyrrhizin, one of the herb's eight anti-viral compounds, acts to inhibit the process involved in viral duplication. It prevents the penetration of the virus into the healthy cells and even stops genetic reproduction. The compounds in licorice boost interferon levels and makes it very difficult for the herpes virus to survive.[2]

Try taking 1,000 to 2,000 milligrams of powdered licorice root in capsule form three times a day

The Miracle of Licorice

when there is an outbreak or if other symptoms of the herpes virus occurs. Make sure you speak with your physician before doing this. Pregnant women should not do this without their physician's consent.

Licorice root has been given much attention as a possible treatment for HIV infection. Research informs us that the herb's active ingredients, glycyrrhizin and glycyrrhetinic acid, can stop a number of processes involved in the virus duplication. It has been found that both compounds stimulate the release of the immune system chemical interferon. Interferon is our body's built-in-virus fighter.[3] Licorice root has the ability of preventing the viral DNA and RNA from attaching to the cell walls. When this occurs, white blood cells called macrophages and natural killer cells are called upon to fight an even strong defense against this odious virus. Licorice does help in preventing the virus from penetrating cells and altering their genetic material.

According to *Prevention* Magazine's health book, *Nature's Medicines*, a study of 16 HIV-positive patients received 150 to 225 milligrams of pure glycyrrhizin on a daily basis for three to seven years. When the study was concluded, researchers found that not one person who received licorice root developed AIDS, nor did any of the patients show further signs of physical deterioration. Their immune systems were not further compromised by the virus.[4]

In another study, ten HIV patients were given 150 to 225 milligrams of glycyrrhizin daily. After a period of two years not one of them developed AIDS.

It is so necessary to have a doctor's supervision when taking a daily dose of 1,500 milligrams of pure powdered licorice root that contains about 5 percent glycyrrhetinic acid. There must be extreme caution in taking such doses of this root since there could be definite negative side effects. As I said earlier, if you should be taking this root in capsule form for more than four to six weeks, the root could cause sodium and water retention, potassium depletion and even high blood pressure. Never take licorice if you have high blood pressure or kidney disease.

There are several other herbs that also assist in HIV retardation. Turmeric can halt HIV replication in numerous ways. This is the spice that gives curry its pungent flavor. The active ingredient in turmeric is a very versatile anti-viral herb called curcumin.[5] This herb gives turmeric its yellow coloration when being used in cooking.

Curcumin is an antioxidant that is 300 times more powerful than vitamin E.[6] The properties of curcumin are very antioxidant and protect the DNA from the ravages of this horrible virus.

Studies done at Harvard Medical School have shown that turmeric prevented the reproduction of HIV by blocking a specific gene that activates the virus that causes it to spread. Other studies have proven that it can inhibit some of the steps that lead to the reproduction of HIV.[7]

Continuous research shows us the miracle of God's natural herbal products. There are literally thousands of herbs that can aid in healing and recovery, but they must be used with discretion and caution. Always seek the counsel of a practitioner of herbalism before starting a program of healing.

Chapter Fourteen

God's Natural Healing for Asthma

Asthma is an ever-increasing health problem all over the world, especially in America and Western Europe. It is growing at a very rapid rate, which is giving the world health community a good deal of grave concern. In the case of asthma, the lungs become oversensitive to certain triggers such as airborne allergens, allergens, exercise, cold air, emotional stress and various foods. When an asthma attack occurs, breathing passages are narrowed, making precious oxygen very scarce. Common symptoms are spasms in the bronchial tubes that cause tightening in the chest and fits of coughing. If the inflammation should linger in the lungs, the person will develop wheezing-type symptoms.

Miracle Herbal Cures

The common approach to treating chronic asthma is to prescribe medication that is inhaled directly so the medication can reach the lungs' air sacs. These drugs do work, but often have various kinds of side effects.

It is imperative, before taking any natural supplements, that you seek the counsel of a good physician. Do not stop taking your asthma medications unless your physician says you can!

Herbs are effective and offer a gentle non-drug alternative. The following have proven to be an impressive means of treatment.

Angelica *(A. atropurpurea)* has been used for hundreds of years to fight flu and the common cold. This herb was used during the Great Plague of Europe. A Catholic monk said he was visited by an angel in his dreams and was told that this herb would cure the plague.[1] This herb was used in a tonic (mixed with water and nutmeg) and administered twice daily to the sick and dying during the great plague.

Angelica also can improve digestion when taken in small amounts. It has been used for digestive, heartburn, gas and bronchial problems.

Prior to World War I, people chewed on the root of Angelica thinking that this would prevent the dreaded influenza that was killing millions of people.

Angelica helps in some cases of asthma since it can open the bronchial tubes. At the same time this herb will be invigorating when taken systematically. It creates a sense of well being and gives individuals energy and vitality.

For hundreds of years this herb was used to treat various types of heart disease and lower blood pressure. It is best taken as a tea, two cups daily, and mixed with a little honey since it is somewhat bitter.

Pregnant women should not take large amounts of this herb. It can cause uterine contractions and should not be taken if there is excessive bleeding.

Another herb that has been successful for hundreds of years in treating various aliments is anise. The Romans used anise *(Pimpinella anisum)* as a flavoring in cooking. Not only was it enjoyed, but it also aided in digestion. The ancient custom of wedding cakes started with the Romans using anise in their cakes. The custom has lasted for hundreds of years and even to this day the herb is used as flavoring in all kinds of pastries, candies and even cough medications. The Romans also chewed anise early in the morning to avoid bad breath.

This herb is used in numerous preparations to improve the taste and flavor of countless natural medications. Anise also stimulates the female glands by controlling estrogen levels.[2] Western European herbalists recommend this herb for treating asthma, coughs and bronchitis. Modern science has shown that anise contains creosol and alpha-pinene, which loosen bronchials secretions, making it much easier to clear these tubes.

Other studies have shown that anise works as a stimulate for the heart, liver, brain and lungs.[3] Anise oil will help alleviate the symptoms of emphysema. Again, anise must be used with caution since it is a powerful herb and could have adverse reactions in certain people.

Miracle Herbal Cures

Both cocoa and coffee help stop asthma attacks. Contrary to popular opinion, cocoa is a chocolaty-tasting substance that is actually good for you. Two chemicals, caffeine and theobromine, give cocoa its great healing potential. Cocoa contains only 10 to 20 percent of caffeine that you find in coffee, so it provides for gentle stimulation.

A standard treatment for asthma is theophylline, which is found especially in inhalers. It is interesting to note that both caffeine and theobromine are chemically related to theophylline. This wonderful herb helps open the air passages in the lungs.

It is recommended that those suffering from asthma should take two cups of cocoa a day. Use about two heaping teaspoons in a cup of hot water and sweeten to taste.

Many people enjoy coffee because of its taste but at the same time it has about 120 milligrams of caffeine per cup, which is much higher than having a cup of cocoa. Even doctors recommend drinking coffee when an asthma attacks occurs.

It is necessary to use wisdom in drinking coffee since it has side effects. Having more than two cups a day may give you the jitters and cause an increase in your blood pressure. It elevates your cholesterol and heart rate. Too much caffeine causes insomnia and irritability so drink it with much caution.

Ginkgo has been known for hundreds of years as an aid in stopping bronchial attacks. The healing action of this herb is its ability to block the action of a natural body substance called platelet activation factor (PAF).[4] (See chapter 4-"High Blood

Pressure and Blood Cleansing") This particular substance plays a major role in many biological processes including organ transplant rejection, blood flow and the formation of blood clots in arteries that may induce heart attacks and strokes.[5] PAF is a major player in asthma attacks. Ginkgo prevents bronchial construction since it blocks the action of PAF.

Ginkgo is available in countless stores across the country. Try to obtain the purest form available. It may cost a little more, but the herb's action will be definitely noticed.

Another aid in the battle against asthma is parsley *(Petroselinum sativum)*. The ancient Greeks and Romans used this lovely herb (leaves) as a flavoring and garnish for their foods. Today, parsley is not valued for its medicinal purposes but used primarily as decoration. Parsley is full of chlorophyll and is excellent as a natural breath sweetener.

In the Middle Ages, parsley became popular in countless herbal medicines. It was used to cure liver and kidney diseases. The ancients used parsley to heal kidney stones and gallstones.

It has been used with much success in providing essential nutrients in cleansing a toxic kidney. Parsley acts as a blood purifier while providing the healthful nutritional material necessary for tissue homeostasis of the urinary system. Parsley is truly a healing balm to the urinary tract making urination much easier.[6] This marvelous herb is a very good diuretic and acts as a laxative.

Urination can become painful and incomplete due to an enlarged prostate.[7] It is known that

Miracle Herbal Cures

parsley is the diuretic of choice since it helps open the urethra making urination easier.

Parsley roots are far more potent than the leaves. Medications made from the parsley root increase the functioning of the liver and spleen. Clinical physicians in Europe have known for more than one hundred years that parsley root is most effective in treating certain liver diseases. This herb also helps in dissolving, and even passing, gallstones and kidney stones.[8]

Parsley should not be used during pregnancy since it can cause an irritation to the uterine membrane and other discomfort to the womb. It also can induce labor. In Europe, parsley is used with a nursing mother to help wean her child from breastfeeding.

Parsley also can reduce high blood pressure and increase the depth of respiration. It is especially good for asthma patients since it aids in the respiration movement.

Parsley is an all-around good tonic for blood vessels, capillaries and arterioles. It helps with blood flow by aiding expansion of arteries and veins of one's body.

SOME HERBS TO AVOID IF YOU HAVE ASTHMA

It is obvious why people today are becoming more and more interested in using herbs. Impersonal doctors, the bureaucratic mess of managed health care systems and soaring prescription costs have led many to return to God's method of healing—natural remedies. The American Association of Poison Control Centers shows that

500 people die from medical drugs for every person killed by an herbal remedy. So it makes sense to try herbal remedies.

We definitely know that herbal remedies promote natural healing. By in large, herbs are very safe but the wrong combination of them or even too many of them can be detrimental to the human body. There are certain herbs that can cause harm if they are misused.

Just because herbs are natural and come from plants does not automatically make them safe. They have the power to help in the healing process by stimulating the human body, but they must be used with caution. Herbs should be used with precisely the same caution used for prescribed medications. Please be advised that all herbs are powerful and can be dangerous if not used wisely.

Before taking any herbs for asthma or for other diseases, learn about them and consult a naturopathic physician or an herbalist. Educate yourself about herbs. Most herbs are very safe, but there are some that can damage the internal organs and even cause death.

Chaparral has been used by Native Americans for hundred of years with great success. Their medicine men know about this herb. Given in small amounts, it has the ability to shrink certain tumors, but it must not be used without the care of a physician since it can cause death. Chaparral contains the chemical NGDA, and the Food and Drug Administration has given sufficient warning that this herb can cause irreparable liver damage. It also aids allergy sufferers and in some cases asthma patients, but again, it must never be used without the care of a physician.

Coltsfoot is another herb used in Europe for coughs, asthma and other respiratory ailments. There are those who use it for superficial cuts and wounds. However, this herb contains dangerous chemicals that can cause liver damage if used unwisely. Coltsfoot is banned in Canada for any type of treatment.

Lobelia is an herb used as an expectorant since the active ingredients loosens secretions in the respiratory tract. It helps expel congestion and improves breathing. It has been prescribed for centuries for pneumonia, asthma and bronchitis.

The problem with Lobelia is its chemical make-up, which resembles nicotine and has been used as a smoking deterrent. This herb is very safe when used at a safe level, taking too much could cause severe nausea and vomiting. In large dosages it can depress breathing, cause a rapid heart beat and, in severe cases, lead to coma or death.

It is best to know about these herbs that have been used in the past for asthma. Do not take any of these without your physician's consent. Knowledge is power—use it to arm yourself with all the facts about herbs.

Chapter Fifteen

God's Cure for the Common Cold

The common cold needs no introduction. The only cure known at this time for the cold is time—eight days to be exact. The best thing to do is alleviate the symptoms of wheezing, spluttering, sneezing and running nose. By easing the symptoms, the entire body is better able to relax and get the rest needed to overcome this nuisance.

So many over-the-counter cold medications are sold every year, but the truth of the matter is that they really all work about the same. The problem we have with these products is the side effects they produce. The major ingredient of most of them is aspirin.

Herbs do not work as effectively as prescription medications, but they certainly enhance the

Miracle Herbal Cures

immune system and speed the healing process. There are numerous herbs available to help with the common cold. Here are a few.

Cayenne or Capsicum *(Capsicum annum)* comes from a fruit family. The activity of the herb in this family is measured by its heat content. Consequently, BTU (British Thermal Unit) ratings are ascribed to the herb.

This herb first became known in Europe when Christopher Columbus returned from the New World. The plant gets its name from a Greek word meaning "to bite." If you have ever taken cayenne, you know it certainly has a bite.

Cayenne was known for hundreds of years in Africa, India and South America, but was not known in Europe until the return of Columbus. North American Indians used cayenne for its stimulating benefits. Navajo Indians, in particular, used the herb to help wean their children.

Cayenne (or Capsicum) is used as a catalyst in numerous herbal combinations. It promotes effective absorption of the combination.[1] It has been known for centuries as an effective means of producing HCL, which will increase the body's ability to better digest food in the stomach. Capsicum is known by herbalists to be a "catalyst."

Today there is a medicinal cream on the market known as "Capsaicin" that helps relieve the symptoms of osteoarthritis and rheumatoid arthritis. This cream, when rubbed on the skin gives hours of precious relief from the pain.

Capsicum has the propensity to promote perspiration. If you are one of those people who like to eat hot peppers you know exactly what these peppers can do. People in tropical climates enjoy hot dishes since it encourages perspiration, which is the body's means of cooling itself.

Cayenne increases "thermogenesis," which is the burning of fat.[2] This herb combines with others containing caffeine to encourage fat burning, and it actually works! At the same time capsicum will stimulate the circulatory system by increasing blood flow.

Cayenne is red in color because it has a very high vitamin A content. Vitamin A is absolutely needed for night vision, growth, cellular activity, reproduction and boosting the immune system.

This herb is excellent in preventing heart disease by normalizing blood pressure, and it aids in preventing stroke and even heart attacks. Placing cayenne under the tongue while a person is experiencing shock or a heart attack will lessen the effects of both.

It may sound very strange but cayenne used in moderation will actually assist in healing stomach ulcers. Herbalists also use the herb as a poultice for almost any inflammation.

Cayenne is also useful in treating colds and flus. Its properties help remove impurities from the stomach and bowels and is effective in the tissue rebuilding of those two organs.[3]

Cayenne is loaded with nutrients such as vitamin C, iron, calcium, phosphorus and B-complex vitamins. Either in capsule or tea form, this herb heats up the body and forces the person to sweat out the toxins.

It helps with asthma attacks. By placing a very tiny amount under the tongue during the attack, it can open the restricted bronchial tubes, which in turn helps alleviate heavy breathing.

Boneset *(Eupatorium perfoliatum)* has been used in Germany and other European countries for hundreds of years to treat colds and flus. This herb is effective in treating flus characterized by body aches and fever.

In Germany, this herb is sold over the counter alongside other cold and flu medication. Research suggests that one of the components of Boneset will consume foreign agents since it encourages the production of white blood cells. Herbalists in Europe use it to treat infectious diseases. Although its name would rather indicate otherwise, it is not used for the treatment of bones.

During the American Civil War, Boneset was given to troops on both sides not only to cure the flu or cold, but as a tonic to keep them healthy and well. During the nineteenth century, Boneset tea was used in the United States as a home remedy for treating colds and flus.

A word of warning about eating fresh Boneset: in high doses it contains a toxic chemical causing nausea, vomiting, weakness and muscle tremors. In rare cases, it could cause coma or even death if taken in too large amounts.

Elderberry *(Sambucus. spp.,)* has been a traditional gypsy cold remedy for countless years. Most herbalists praise the effects of this herb since it is loaded with vitamins A, B and C.

There is a belief among many herbalists that the elder flower tree provided the wood for the cross upon which Jesus Christ was crucified. Herbalists use elder flower for detoxifying the body at a cellular level.[4] It increases circulation and promotes sweating. In many cases, sweating is needed to rid the system of poisons.

Not only does the elder flower help in reducing the symptoms of colds, it also has an anti-catarrhal action. There is no better herb to use in the first stages of a cold than the elder flower. This herb may be used both internally and externally for various ailments.

Elderberry tea has been used for numerous centuries as a folk remedy for colds, coughs and flus. The Pennsylvania Shakers knew of the medicinal properties of this herb. Elderberry tea has been used for countless infirmities with good to moderate success.

In some instances the tea works far better than prescriptions medications. Just recently scientists have found that the herb contains viburnic acid, a chemical that induces perspiration, which is beneficial in various kinds of flus, colds and bronchitis.

Echinacea *(Echinacea purpurea)* has been around for a very long time. It is known as a very good blood purifier and some have called it the "king of blood purifiers." Naturopathic doctors like this herb very much since it is a natural antibiotic and a very good alternative to other herbs. Echinacea is most useful in the treatment of vertigo. This herb also has been used throughout the centuries to help cure bronchitis and similar infections.

Extensive scientific studies done in Europe and America indicate that this herb acts with an antibiotic cortisone behavior. It helps with the synovial membrane between all joints, supports collagen

Miracle Herbal Cures

healing, provides hytaluronic acid protection, promotes wound healing, aids in the production of interferon and stimulates the production of T-cell lymphocytes. It is believed to also help in tumor suppression.

The active compounds in echinacea aid in destroying bacterial and viral invaders. The herb is most potent in enhancing the immune system. Consequently, it is very important for colds and flus since it helps to build up the immune system to fight the invading virus or bacteria. It should be noted that there are no side effects from the use of this herb.

Herbalists believe echinacea functions very well in fighting glandular infections and ailments. It also is effective in treating strep throat with the addition of antibiotics.

Echinacea also helps block the receptor site of the virus on the cell membrane, which will aid in fighting infection.

This is another God-given weapon in the arsenal of herbs to fight colds and flus. Again, like all herbs it must be used with caution. Do not exceed the recommended dosages.

Eucalyptus *(Eucalyptus gloulus)* is native to Australia and there are over 500 different species of Eucalyptus. It was Australian Aborigines who first discovered the remarkable tree. They also discovered the oil of the Eucalyptus called "eucalyptol," which is used in numerous medicinal preparations.

Eucalyptus has been used externally as a deodorant, but is far more effective in treating discharging wounds, ulcers, and gangrenous and cancerous lesions. It has proven itself to be a great asset in the herbalist's pharmacy.

This herb is most helpful in treating flus, pneumonia and the common cold. It is the oil of the herb that has such healing power. It must be noted that the oil should never be ingested over a long period of time since it has great difficulty in leaving the body. The kidneys are strained if too much oil is ingested.

Eucalyptus is found in many over-the-counter cold preparations and cough drops. Vicks Vap-O-Rub, for instance, has the distinctive fragrance of Eucalyptus oil. These healing vapors can temporarily relieve a stuffy nose and a sluggish brain.

All of the herbs mentioned in this chapter have profound healing properties. Again, they must be used with caution; never exceed the recommended dosage.

Chapter Sixteen

God's Natural Relief From Stress

Heavy traffic, difficult work situations, marital problems, rebellious teenagers, illness and personal injury can all add up to big-time stress. All of these can give you a headache you won't forget and even knock you off your feet. Without some type of relief, you may feel that each morning you get out of bed is the beginning of a new tragedy instead of a new beginning.

Making fun of stress is not going to help you out of it. Stress is a very serious thing. When we're filled with tension and anxiety, the adrenal glands, located above the kidneys, push out stress hormones such as adrenaline and cortisol, which will give your body a new burst of energy that it needs to escape the chaos of the day. Long-term stress

Miracle Herbal Cures

causes chronically high levels of these hormones, which eventually weaken your immune system, tax your heart and blood vessels. You will experience constant fatigue and make you susceptible to all kinds of disease.

Fortunately, there are dietary and lifestyle changes that can alleviate a lot of stress and get you on the road to renewed health. Having twenty to thirty minutes of aerobic exercise at least three to five times weekly will aid greatly in stress reduction. Weight lifting and/or brisk walking also will help reduce the stress factor in your life.

It is so important to limit the amount of caffeine, alcohol, high-fat foods and white sugar in your daily diet. It is a fact that caffeine and alcohol can raise the levels of stress hormones in the blood. At the same time, your brain chemistry can be affected negatively. When an individual limits the amount of good nutritious food in his diet, he actually lowers the amount of necessary vitamins and minerals found in good foods. This in turn weakens the immune system since the body is being depleted of important nutrients.

Make changes as soon as possible and get a nutritional assessment to know exactly what you need in your diet.

Remember, it is very important to be conscious of keeping your immune system in good shape. By doing so, you will prevent stress-induced diseases.

To help fight stress, God has given us some very good herbs. Perhaps the best known one is Ginseng *(Panax schinseng)*. Ginseng can restore vitality, boost energy, reduce fatigue, improve mental and physical performance. At the same time this herb can protect the body from the negative effects of stress. It has been proven that while taking ginseng, our initial reaction to stress is most likely to be less intense. Ginseng is known as a tonic for the adrenal glands since it tones and maintains one's overall health.

Ginseng gets its name *Panax* from the Greek word *panacea*, which means "all healing." Panax is taken from the Greek word *Pan*, which signifies power and when it is combined with the Greek word *akos* or *ills*, it implies the plant is a cure for all illnesses. Of course, this is not totally accurate. But it certainly does help with energy levels and does boost performance. The Chinese use ginseng in countless preparations. The name *ginseng* was given to the plant by early Chinese herbalists with its meaning "man plant" since the root resembles that of masculine-type figure.[1]

Ginseng is used worldwide by athletes to boost performance and it is used also as an aphrodisiac. It has excellent properties for the healing of the prostate gland. Women must use it with caution because ginseng aids in the production of testosterone. Women should use ginseng for only a short period of time.

We know that ginseng is an excellent energy booster, but it also assists with stress. The Chinese have been using ginseng for over 5,000 years with great success. In actuality it belongs to a class of compounds called adaptogens, which means it normalizes the body when it is out of balance. For example, if you are suffering from high blood pressure, it will lower it over a period of time. Again, if you are having problems with low blood pressure,

Miracle Herbal Cures

it will raise it up in a short period of time. Ginseng is beneficial for the entire body.

The herb has been used for the digestive system since it helps in the recovery of various illnesses and is combined with other tonics for building strength in the infirmed.

This miraculous herb is considered by some herbalists to be the most effective adaptogen of all tonic herbs.[2] The herb contains germanium, which provides energy for all bodily systems. It aids in the regeneration of the body if it has been subjected to measurable amounts of stress and fatigue. It assists in building bodily strength. Ginseng is excellent for the male reproductive system and also helps in circulation. It is known by the Chinese to aid in brain and memory functions. In order to enjoy the total benefits of this herb it must be taken over a period of several months. Again, women must not take ginseng for a prolonged period of time. Only a few weeks is advisable for women since it can cause masculinization of the female body.

Ginseng gives people more energy, promotes good brain function and builds up cells throughout the entire body. It has been known to raise blood pressure when an individual is suffering from low blood pressure. It also has the opposite effect on individuals suffering from high blood pressure.

Ginseng helps fight fatigue and depression by aiding in the elimination of stress. This will then assist in improving the well being of the entire body. At the same time, ginseng has a long history of improving normal adrenal flow from the adrenal glands.[3] Thus, it also is very effective in combating male impotence.

Ginseng attacks free radicals in the body. Consequently, it aids in slowing down the aging process.

Individuals do vary in response to ginseng. Asian ginseng is the most popular in the United States. It is always best to start off with a lower dosage. More may be added after a short period of time if required.

Kava Kava has an analgesic sedative effect and has been used successfully in the treatment of rheumatic complaints. It aids in reducing stress, alleviating insomnia and helps to calm the nerves. The natives of Tahiti made a very strong tonic from Kava Kava and have even used it as a stimulant in small doses.

Kava Kava has the ability to relax the muscles. It is helpful in increasing flexibility and influencing the motor units of the nervous system.[4] It is very effective in reducing muscle tension and helps skeleton alignment.

Kava Kava is very effective in relaxing the urinary tract. It has been used to treat bladder infections since it has an antiseptic property about it.

It is considered a stress buster. After taking Kava, results will be noticed within thirty to sixty minutes. If you are expecting a stressful situation Kava may be taken to preempt the stress. It will help you wind down if you've had a heavy stress day.

The secret behind the remarkable herb is its anxiety-reducing effect on the brain, according to most herbalists. Kava contains a group of chemicals called "kavalactones" that help with the anti-anxiety effects. These chemicals act on the part of the brain that is the center of emotions.

Kava is non-addictive and does not lose its effectiveness over time. The mind remains alert and sharp even though it is taken during the early part of the day.

It is best to take smaller doses in the beginning. If you don't feel any change when taking 40 to 70 milligrams of Kavalactones two or three times a day then increase the dosage. Take an extra capsule and you should feel the effects.

Passion flower is another herb that helps reduce stress. This herb contains three tranquilizing chemicals and is very good as a natural sedative.

While herbs are great for adults, herbs should not be given to children under two years of age. Older children and individuals over sixty-five should be given weaker preparations. The dosage may increase later if the body is able to handle the chemicals found in the herbs.

Remember that herbs are powerful medicines and must be used cautiously When starting an herbal program, find out what the herb can do and the possible side effects. Always consult your physician before starting an herbal program. If your family doctor is not well acquainted with herbs, then see a good naturopathic physician.

Chapter Seventeen

Natural Help for Arthritis

Arthritis is chronic inflammation of the joints. People who suffer from this condition can tell you how very painful it is. The joints become inflamed and swollen making normal functioning most difficult.

There are several types of arthritis: osteoarthritis, rheumatoid arthritis and gout. According to the American Arthritis Foundation, it is believed that approximately 60 to 65 million people in this country suffer from this disease.

The most common type is osteoarthritis. It is best known as the "wear and tear" arthritis that bothers at least 40 million Americans. The cumulative effects of stress and usage of the joints cause enormous problems as people get older. The knees,

Miracle Herbal Cures

hips, feet and hands are most affected since in one way or another they carry so much weight. It is this factor that further complicates an already difficult disease.

Rheumatoid arthritis is perhaps the most painful of the three types of arthritis. It is a chronic inflammatory condition that causes a great deal of swelling as well as destruction of the joints involved. This arthritis will effect the entire body but especially the joints. It is commonly called an "autoimmune disease," which means that the disease itself will attack and destroy otherwise perfectly healthy cells of the joints such as the hands, feet, wrists, ankles and knees. It is believed that as many as 14 million Americans suffer from this dreaded malady.

King Henry the VIII suffered from gout. We often see cartoon caricatures of King Henry and his big right toe. Gout is definitely a form of arthritis caused by an excess of uric acid in the blood and lymph fluids. This leads to the formation of hard crystals that settle in the joints, especially the toes. The pain is most vicious. Attacks of gout are often triggered by excessive consumption of certain foods, especially those rich in fats and alcohol. Red wine is notorious in causing gout attacks.

The standard treatment for most kinds of arthritis in America is non-steroidal anti-inflammatory drugs (NSAIDs). Aspirin has been used for years since it is an effective means of controlling pain.

Aspirin comes to us from the bark of the white willow tree. It is possible to obtain white willow bark tablets from your local health food stores.

There is a very good reason for taking white willow tablets since the NSAIDs drugs will cause the progression of arthritis and joint destruction. Aspirin has been prescribed for the relief of arthritic pain and even thinning the blood, but it does have serious side effects. It can cause stomach and intestinal ulcers, which could cause hemorrhage and even death. Aspirin with prolonged usage can cause health problems that you really don't need. There are numerous herbal preparations that can be taken without any harmful side effects. These will tone and strengthen the body and improve general good health.

If you are fighting a battle with arthritis it is so important to examine your diet. It should be low in fat and high in fiber and should consist of a wide variety of fruits, vegetables and whole grains. Several studies have shown that eating a vegetarian diet is most beneficial for rheumatoid arthritis patients. This diet could be helpful for osteoarthritis, too.

At the same time, certain foods can provoke allergic reactions and even aggravate arthritis. The nightshade family of foods such as wheat, corn, milk and other dairy products will cause reactions. Vegetables such as tomatoes, potatoes and eggplant also can trigger an arthritic attack. It would be very wise to be tested to see if you have allergic reactions to nightshade foods.

If you are suffering from arthritis you should start eating more fish, perhaps up to four times a week. Research indicates that high content of EPA (eicosapentaenoic acid) in cold water fish such as salmon, sardines, herring and mackerel will reduce

Miracle Herbal Cures

inflammation from arthritis. Flaxseed oil and evening primrose oil supply very similar benefits and should be taken on a daily basis.

Some of the best herbs for arthritis are the following:

As we have studied previously, Angelica *(A. atropurpurea)* has many healing properties, among them is the ability to treat arthritis. Angelica has been used in Asia for centuries as a traditional arthritis remedy. In Japan, researchers have discovered it contains anti-inflammatory compounds.

The traditional herb Black Cohosh *(Cimicifuga racemosa)* can be used for the treatment of arthritis because it helps relieve the inflammation.

When the herb is in blossom it gives off a strong aroma that makes it effective as insect repellent.[1] Its Latin name *Cimicifuga* means "bug repellent." The Native American culture has used this herb over the centuries for snake bites. It has also been useful in the treatment of bee stings.

The Puritans used this herb for treating yellow fever, malaria, fevers and numerous other ailments. But this herb must not be taken if you're pregnant or suffering from kidney problems. The herb can induce labor pains that could result in miscarriage.

Burdock *(Arctium lappa)* has a long history of being a blood purifier. The herb helps build up the body since it is full of nutrients.

Burdock can be used during pregnancy since it is mineral rich. It has a hormone in it that assists the body in balancing all of its systems. It promotes the flow of urine and aids in riding the body of toxins by causing it to sweat. It is known in herbal folklore as an excellent remedy for reducing the inflammation of arthritis.

You are able to purchase this herb in capsule form. Do not exceed the recommended dosage. It also can be taken in drop form, but do not exceed 10 to 20 drops daily.

Chamomile *(Anthemis nobilis-Roman)* is commonly known by the Greeks as the "ground apple."[2] Chamomile is derived from the Greek work *kamai,* meaning "on the ground" and *melon* meaning "apple".[3] The plant grows low to the ground and has a delightful fragrance, but a bitter taste.

The herb has been used for centuries to help one relax and sleep. It also relieves bowel and digestive difficulties.

Chamomile has been used with much success in relieving the pain of arthritis. Studies in animals indicated a reduced amount of inflammation after it has been administered.

The herb is available just about everywhere today. It may be used as a tea without potential digestive upsets. However, chamomile can cause allergic reactions in those who are sensitive to Ragweed or other varieties of Chrysanthemum.

Devil's Claw *(Harpagophytum procumbens)* is grown in the Namibian Steppes and the nearby Kalahari Desert of South Africa. I first became aware of the healing herb while living in northern England when it was recommended to me by an herbalist for relief from arthritic pain. To my amazement it did the job quite well. It gets its name from the thorny, barbed claw arrangements of the seed pod.[4] Its use has been known in France and Germany as an anti-inflammatory for over 250 years.

Miracle Herbal Cures

It is amazingly comparable to cortisone and phenylbutazone. These are powerful prescription drugs that have some serious side effects. Devil's Claw may be taken in capsule form one to three per day depending upon the size of the dosage. Stop immediately if there are digestive problems with this herb.

Ginger *(Zingiber officinale)* became very popular during the sixteenth century. The Spaniards were the first to introduce this plant to the New World. By the late 1890s England was importing over five million pounds of the root. They saw the great effects of this herb not just for spicing, but for medicinal purposes. Stomachaches and digestive disorders respond almost immediately after taking the tea.

It is believed by many that ginger root can help prevent strokes and even hardening of the arteries. There have been several studies conducted at Cornell University Medical College, which indicate that the active ingredient, Gingerol, has the propensity of preventing small strokes. Gingerol has shown itself to inhibit an enzyme that causes clotting of the cells.[5]

My grandfather, George Washington McCann, used ginger on numerous occasions for his many patients with great success. At the same time he proposed using ginger as an anti-inflammatory for those who came to him suffering from arthritis.

Ginger does a wonderful job of relieving pain and preventing unnecessary harmful health problems. Ginger also reduces high cholesterol and assists in cholesterol regulation by improving blood circulation and preventing platelets from clotting. It truly is one of those herbs with numerous benefits for many diseases.

Another great benefit of ginger is that it alleviates menstrual cramps for women. It brings great relief from excessive menstrual flow and increases the output of urine. It should be taken as a hot tea. It also is great for pregnant women since ginger is full of wonderful minerals and has been known to help alleviate morning sickness.

We do know that ginger helps relieve the pain of rheumatoid arthritis for those who have not received relief from conventional therapy. It has been suggested to take one to five grams of powered ginger in capsule form for pain relief. Again, this should be done under your physician's directions to prevent toxic poisoning.

While arthritis can be painful, there are great God-given herbs to cure us and improve the quality of our lives.

Chapter Eighteen

Putting It All Together

> "He causeth the grass to grow for the cattle, and herbs for the service of Man" (Ps. 104:14).

Herbs have been known and used for hundreds of years. Because they are natural, they have few side effects compared to orthodox medicine. Herbs comprise much of the realm of plants found on planet earth.

We find herbs being used in Indian ayuvedic medicine and in Chinese medicine alongside acupuncture and other modalities. Herbs still play a very important role both in the spiritual and ecological healing forces of the North American Indian. They are being used today in highly scientific and technological approaches of modern pharmacy and western medicine.

Modern so-called "orthodox" medicine has its roots in the use of countless herbs. Until about sixty years ago, almost all entries in the pharmacopoeia describing the manufacture of drugs indicate an herbal origin. It only has been since the development of modern chemistry that the use of herbs has diminished. Nevertheless, modern medicines still have their origin in the plant world.

Herbal medicine in its primary sense recognizes mankind as an expression of life caused by God, enlivened with a life force. Herbs work in conjunction with this life force bringing about health in a most natural way. Remember, herbs work with the whole being, not just with symptoms.

Herbs are full of all kinds of ingredients that work in a synergistic manner. This outstanding fact far exceeds the considerations of chemotherapy that would not even take this into consideration.

There is such a profound move today in America for self-healing, which can be viewed as a great blessing or a curse. There are numerous factors to take into consideration before one should start doctoring himself. The term "self-healing" has its roots in the Greek word *holos,* the same word that has given us "whole" and "holistic." We understand that healing is the expression of wholeness and that health is wholeness. The experiences and expression of wholeness must come from within the individual; it will never come from an outer source such as a teacher or doctor. Herbs initiate the wholeness expression within the ailing individual. Biblical healing and divine health are based

Putting It All Together

upon the teaching of the Bible. The Bible is full of herbal remedies and their uses in conjunction with various diseases.

When the spirit, soul and body of man are in unity, health then becomes an expression of an integrated being. Such a person is in tune with his heavenly Father and in awareness of his inner person. Our emotions, thought life and spiritual awareness are important to our health as is the existent state of our organs within the body tissues. Whether we are interested in living healthy or regaining health, the spiritual condition of the soul must never be neglected. We are obligated to keep in mind the spiritual factors involved in health and healing.

Healing comes from within the individual as he recognizes his spiritual awareness. When I speak of our awareness I am speaking of our relationship to Jesus Christ. We can seek aid from medical doctors, herbalists, naturopathic physicians or other such experts, but the responsibility of our healing is our own.

We have been so conditioned that our healing belongs to someone else, such as a family practitioner. This is just not the case. The family doctor can assist you, but the responsibility of being well and whole is up to *you*. Herbs will aid in this glorious process, but healing still comes from within your inner man. It is so important at this point to stress the need of a right relationship with our heavenly Father if we're seeking any manner of healing.

Healing is releasing the inner energy within the body itself. If the body is given good nutrition,

Miracle Herbal Cures

pure water and good air, herbs will facilitate a true healing. Remember that herbs only facilitate a healing. It is the body's life force working in conjunction with the spirit and soul that releases the energy to bring about the desired result.

Indeed, at times herbs do appear to be really miraculous. At the same time, there may be a need to use other modalities to accomplish a lasting cure. Do not limit yourself just to herbs though they often produce remarkable results.

For those seeking a healing from complicated diseases, do not forget the need of being in touch with the Holy Spirit within you. Healing can come about as we are in touch with our inner man. But the inner man must be in touch with the Holy Spirit before the miracle of healing can occur. Herbs are only a means of aiding the body while the spirit and soul of man need to properly relate to Almighty God.

Prayer is so essential in complicated cases of healing. Prayer allows our spirits to open and receive from our Lord. Miracles come only as we are in touch with God's Spirit.

In all that has been said, our inner person must be free so that the body's powers of wholeness and regeneration might produce the healing results. No matter how sincere we might be about getting well, there will necessitate a lifestyle change. If your lifestyle is not filled with good things, or your eating habits are horrible, you will not get well. There can be no neglect of the spiritual aspects of our lives for it is in a right relationship with God through Jesus Christ that fosters healing and even a miracle.

Putting It All Together

Remember we have the power of choice. We can change if we so desire. We have a free will. If we are not able to change our outer situation, we certainly can change the inner man by prayer and meditation. Herbs are an aid in healing. They are not the means of healing. They only release the body's own forces of recuperation.

The way you see yourself before God and man is so very important. Your beliefs can limit the healing power within yourself or they can release the power of healing within your inner person. Examine your belief system. Are you in a right relationship with God? Who is Jesus Christ to you? At the same time the way we see ourselves can have a dynamic impact on our health. If you have a poor self-image, healing then becomes a more difficult process. Herbs cannot change your self-image. They can only aid in unlocking the powers within your body.

Look at your relationships. Are you in good standing with those in your work life and personal life? Are you a giving and loving person? All of these aspects can make a tremendous difference in your life. As we create relationships that affirm our loving nature, the potential for healing is more likely. Choose to be kind and loving. Choose loving friends who will support you in your time of need.

The way you live and the house you live in can make a vast difference in seeking your healing. Is your home a place of peace and tranquility or is it a battleground? This could be a constructive force in your healing or it could slow down the healing process.

Herbs possess an astonishing power to heal, but they are not an end in themselves. They assist the

Miracle Herbal Cures

body in releasing its inner powers for healing. Our spiritual life is so vital when one desires to get well. Prayer and God's Word must accompany you on your pilgrimage of healing.

A key to self-healing is love. Love is the means that opens the door of the soul to receive not only from man, but especially from God. Love causes us to become compassionate. The needs of others become more important to us than our own needs. Oftentimes healings are delayed because we're focusing so much attention on our problems or circumstances. True compassion enables you to reach out to others as your love for them becomes more obvious. Compassion sees the world in a whole different light. Did we not see this very principle displayed so effectively in the life of Mother Teresa? Her life was exemplified by her love for Christ and compassion for others.

Herbs can be miraculous. When herbs are coupled with lifestyle changes, healing will ensure. If your desire is to begin self-healing, please see a qualified physician or naturopathic doctor who can oversee your progress. There may be some herbs that you should not be taking while others could be more beneficial. Remember that some combinations of herbs can be toxic and damaging to your body. Again, before starting self-healing, make sure you are under the supervision of one who knows about herbs. Always seek the advice of one trained in herbal medicine.

Herbs can be truly miraculous. Our openness to the Holy Spirit brings the power to release our inner energies and make us whole—body, mind and spirit. Herbs are God's "wonder tonic" that affirm our wholeness as God's Spirit does the rest.

Notes

CHAPTER ONE
GOD'S WAY OF HEALTHY LIVING

1. Philip St. Vincent Brennan, *Bible Health Guide,* (MicroMags, Lantana, FL 1996), 25.
2. Earl Mindell, *Herb Bible, (Simon & Schuster,* New York, NY, 1992), 19.
3. Ibid., 29.
4. Ibid., 29.
5. Ibid., 29.
6. Ibid., 30.

CHAPTER TWO
USING HERBS WISELY

1. Michael Tierra, C.A., N.D., *The Way of Herbs,* (Pocket Books, Simon & Schuster Inc., New York, 1990), 12.
2. Ibid., 14.
3. Ibid., 14.
4. Ibid., 15.
5. Ibid., 17.
6. Ibid., 18.

CHAPTER THREE
STRENGTHENING THE HEART

1. Jack Ritchason, N.D., *The Little Herb Encyclopedia,* (Woodland Health Books, Pleasant Grove, Utah, 1995) 116.
2. Ibid., 116.
3. John Heinerman, *Healing Herbs & Spices,* (Parker

Notes

Publishing Company, West Nyack, N.Y., 1996) 203.
4. Ibid., 204.
5. Jim O'Brien, *Herbal Cures*, (Globe Communi-cations Corp., Boca Raton, FL 1998), 69.
6. John Heinerman, *Healing Herbs & Spices*, 226.
7. Ibid., 342.

CHAPTER FOUR
HIGH BLOOD PRESSURE AND BLOOD CLEANSING

1. Jim O'Brien, *Herbal Cures*, (Globe Communi-cation Corp., Boca Raton, FL 1998), 69.
2. Dian Dincin Buchman, Ph.D., *Herbal Medicine*, (Wings Books, Random House Value Publishing, Inc., New York, 1996), 199.
3. Jack Ritchason, N.D., *The Little Herbal Encyclopedia* (Woodland Health Books, Pleasant Grove, Utah, 1995), 40.
4. Ibid., 40.
5. Ibid., 55.
6. Ibid., 76.
7. Ibid., 260.

CHAPTER FIVE
GOD'S LITTLE LIVER PILLS

1. Charles B. Clayman, M.D., *Encyclopedia of Medicine*, (Random House, New York, 1989), 644.
2. Ibid., 644.
3. Ibid., 644.
4. Ibid., 645.
5. Jack Ritchason N.D., *The Little Herb Encyclopedia*, (Woodland Health Books, Pleasant Grove, Utah, 1995), 147.
6. Ibid., 147.
7. Ibid., 71.
8. Ibid., 72.

CHAPTER SIX
OSTEOPOROSIS: THE CASE OF THE SHRINKING HUMAN

1. Charles B. Clayman, M.D., *Encyclopedia of Medicine*, (Random House, New York, 1989), 756.
2. Ibid., 756.
3. Jack Ritchason, N.D., *The Little Herb Encyclopedia*, (Woodland Health Books, Pleasant Grove, Utah, 1995), 5.

4. Ibid., 121.
5. Carlson Wade, *Magic of Minerals,* (Parker Publishing Company, Inc., West Nyack, N.Y. 1967), 23.
6. Ibid., 18.
7. Ibid., 19.

CHAPTER SEVEN
NEW HOPE FOR THE DIABETIC

1. Charles B. Clayman, M.D., *Encyclopedia of Medicine,* (Random House, New York, 1989), v.s. "Diabetes mellitus."
2. Ibid., v.s. "Diabetes mellitus."
3. Peter R. Rothschild & Dora L. Rothschild, *Non-Medicinal Self-Help Guide,* (Maps Publishing, San Antonio, TX, 1992), 17.
4. Jack Ritchason, N.D., *The Little Herb Encyclopedia,* (Woodland Health Books, Pleasant Grove, Utah, 1995), 127.
5. Ibid., 128.
6. Ibid., 128.
7. Ibid., 107.
8. Ibid., 108.
9. Ibid., 130.
10. Ibid., 131.
11. Peggy Canning, M.A., *Exotic Supplements,* (Margaret H. Canning, Vista, California, 1994), 8.
12. Ibid., 8.

CHAPTER EIGHT
GOD'S NATURAL PROZAC

1. Jean Carper, *Miracle Cures,* (Harper Collins Publishers, New York, 1997), 45.
2. C.M. Hawken, *St. John's Wort,* (Woodland Publishing, Pleasant Grove, Utah, 1997), 13.
3. Ibid., 18.
4. Ibid., 18.
5. Ibid., 19.
6. Ibid., 19.
7. Ibid., 19.
8. Ibid., 22.
9. Ibid., 23.
10. Ibid., 24
11. Ibid., 24.

Notes

CHAPTER NINE
GOD'S MIRACLE CURE FOR THE PROSTATE

1. Jack Ritchason, N.D., *The Little Herb Encyclopedia,* (Woodland Health Books, Pleasant Grove, Utah, 1995), 213.
2. Ibid., 213.
3. Ibid., 213.
4. Jim O'Brien, *Herbal Cures for Common Ailments,* (Globe Communications Corp., Boca Raton, FL), 1988), 73.

CHAPTER TEN
GOD'S NATURAL ASPIRIN

1. Jack Ritchason, N.D., *The Little Herb Encyclopedia,* (Woodland Health Books, Pleasant Grove, Utah, 1995), 87.
2. Ibid., 87.
3. Jean Carper, *Miracle Cures,* (Harper Collins Publishers, New York, 1997), 85.
4. Ibid., 86.
5. Ibid., 88.
6. Ibid., 90.

CHAPTER ELEVEN
GOD'S BEST HERBS FOR ANXIETY

1. Jack Ritchason, N.D., *The Little Herb Encyclopedia,* (Woodland Health Books, Pleasant Grove, Utah, 1995), 166.
2. Ibid., 216.
3. Ibid., 216.

CHAPTER TWELVE
HELPFUL HERBS FOR ALLERGIES

1. Jack Ritchason, N.D., *The Little Herb Encyclopedia,* (Woodland Health Books, Pleasant Grove, Utah, 1995), 81.
2. Ibid., 82.
3. Ibid., 157.
4. Ibid., 152.
5. Ibid., 153.

6. Ibid., 152.

Chapter Thirteen
The Miracle of Licorice

1. Gale Maleskey, *Nature's Medicines,* (Rodale Press, Inc., Emmaus, Pennsylvania, 1999), 369.
2. Ibid., 443.
3. Ibid., 489.
4. Ibid., 489.
5. Ibid., 490.
6. Ibid., 490.
7. Ibid., 490.

Chapter Fourteen
God's Natural Healing for Asthma

1. Jack Ritchason, N.D., *The Little Herb Encyclopedia,* (Woodland Health Books, Pleasant Grove, Utah, 1995), 10.
2. Ibid., 12.
3. Ibid., 12.
4. Jim O'Brien, *Herbal Cures For Common Ailments,* (Globe Communications Corp., Boca Raton, FL, 1998), 37.
5. Ibid., 163.
6. Ibid., 163.
7. Ibid., 163.
8. Ibid., 163.

Chapter Fifteen
God's Cure for the Common Cold

1. Jack Ritchason, N.D., *The Little Herb Encyclopedia,* (Woodland Health Books, Pleasant Grove, Utah, 1995), 44.
2. Ibid., 44.
3. Ibid., 43.
4. Ibid., 78.

CHAPTER SIXTEEN
GOD'S NATURAL RELIEF FROM STRESS

1. Jack Ritchason, N.D., *The Little Herb Encyclopedia*, (Woodland Health Books, Pleasant Grove, Utah, 1995), 101.
2. Ibid., 101.
3. Ibid., 102.
4. Ibid., 129.

CHAPTER SEVENTEEN
NATURAL HELP FOR ARTHRITIS

1. Jack Ritchason, N.D., *The Little Herb Encyclopedia*, (Woodland Health Books, Pleasant Grove, Utah, 1995), 10.
2. Ibid., 52.
3. Ibid., 53.
4. Ibid., 73.
5. Ibid., 97.

Other Books by Dr. Michael McCann

Alternative Therapies for HIV/AIDS
Prescription for Health
Eat Well - Love Well

Videos by Dr. Michael McCann

Video by Dr. McCann

Heart Attack: Prevention and Recovery
Cancer: How to win the war
Chemotherapy or Not
Prostate Cancer
Breast Cancer
PMS and Hormone Balance
What I would do if I had HIV or Aids
Natural Alternative for Prozac and other prescription drug
Diabetes
Pregnancy: What to eat while pregnant
Menopause
Alternatives and Remedies to consider before surgery

Notes

Printed in the United States
1528300004B/406-429